# CORRECTIVE
# LOVE

CONCORDIA
SCHOLARSHIP
Today

# CORRECTIVE
# LOVE

## The Power of Communion
## Discipline

Thomas C. Oden

CPH™
SAINT LOUIS

Copyright © 1995 Concordia Publishing House
3558 S. Jefferson Avenue, St. Louis, MO 63118-3968
Manufactured in the United States of America

Library of Congress Cataloging-in-Publication Data

Oden, Thomas C.
    Corrective love : the power of communion discipline / Thomas C. Oden.
        p.          cm.          —(Concordia scholarship today)
        ISBN 0-570-04803-6
        1. Church discipline. 2. Power of the keys. 3. Church—Holiness. 4. Forgiveness of sins. 5. Confession. 6. Absolution.   I. Title. II. Series.
BV740.027     1995
262´.8—dc20                                                      95-4150

1 2 3 4 5 6 7 8 9 10       04 03 02 01 00 99 98 97 96 95

# Contents

CONTENTS

# Foreword

Like all volumes in the Concordia Scholarship Today series, this book offers insights that relate to current concerns. The assumption is that an analysis and clarification of issues that beset us today, viewed against a broadened and deepened understanding of the Christian faith, will lead us to make considered and responsible applications and in so doing help us to "comprehend the love of God in Christ Jesus" (Eph. 3: 17–19). The primary objective of the Concordia Scholarship Today series is to encourage church professionals and educated Christians to develop the habit of thinking theologically about contemporary issues.

Today, secularism—really practical atheism disguised as a rational worldview—has reached a new stage where it has insidiously weakened or destroyed beliefs, attitudes, and conventions that have sustained civilization for centuries. A new culture has inexorably been replacing the old, largely through the denigration of the transcendent by the media and a popular presupposition that rational people do not take religion seriously.

It has become patently clear that the undermining of cultural values and the seeming inability of American Christians to turn things in the right direction are to a great extent due to the mistaken belief (value) that there is no such thing as objective truth. Not only does everyone supposedly have the right to determine for himself/herself what is truth but also to decide moral truth and, even more basic, whether or not God exists.

Numerous attempts have been made to pinpoint the problems and the moral crisis of our time. Perhaps no one has analyzed and grappled with the basic problems of society more specifically and cogently in the light of Scripture than

Herbert Schlossberg in his classic *Idols for Destruction: Christian Faith and Its Confrontation with American Society*. Now Thomas Oden, also recognizing the same importance of biblical principles and guidance, has immersed himself in the patristic writings, mining them for their timeless gems. He concludes that "the tested language of the ancient church speaks in its own unrelenting ways to modern minds struggling with the follies and limits of modern consciousness."

But Oden does not advocate a return to the Christian classics and the Scriptures because everyone presumably needs a pragmatic crutch of some kind. We are dealing with basic verities. His peregrinations through "Marxist–Freudian-Bultmannian deconstructionism," he confesses, have led him now to "relish poring over the abundant diversity of orthodox Scripture interpretation . . . experiencing a refreshing breeze of classic theological liberation."

Three earlier publications of the author have laid the groundwork for this volume: *Agenda for Theology, After Modernity ... What?*; *Two Worlds: Notes on the Death of Modernity in America and Russia*; and *Requiem: A Lament in Three Movements*. The author states that his "inquiry into post–modern classical Christian consciousness is applied now for the first time deliberately to the questions of confession, discipline, admonition, and the governance of the church."

This volume appears at a time when our world is in crisis. To be sure, it always has been and always will be, but at the moment it seems especially "out of control." While organizations and groups can and should work to relieve some of the symptoms, only *individuals*, moved by the Holy Spirit through the Gospel working individually or collectively, can bring a true measure of relief. *Corrective Love* leads us through the necessary steps from confession to discipline, admonition, and a manageable modus vivendi.

*The Publisher*

# Prelude
# Tending the Garden

With my gardening gloves on, each spring I am again surprised at how clever my particular weeds have become. Some upstart weeds are insidiously resourceful in mimicking my favorite flowers and vegetables. Sometimes when I try to yank weeds wrapped around other favored roots, I inadvertently injure the very plants I am trying to cultivate.

The owner of the field in which tares were sown, Jesus said, was asked by gardeners if he wanted them to *destroy all the weeds*. No, he replied, "because while you are pulling the weeds, you may root up the wheat with them. Let both grow until the harvest" (Matt. 13:29–30). Harvest is final judgment. The weeds are tolerated either when they cannot be distinguished or cannot be removed without injury to the wheat. Until final judgment, wild weeds will be rashly pushing up into the fertile soil set aside for God's green garden.

Distasteful fish will be caught in the dragnet of general proclamation and mass evangelization, which catches all kinds (Matt. 13:47–50). The final sorting out will occur only on the last day. Till then, let God judge. Like the ark, the church houses all sorts, clean and unclean.

Those who chide the church for its lack of holiness are inadvertently pointing toward the church's genuine call to holiness. Efforts of detractors to prove that the church is not holy ironically show that they acknowledge holiness as a valid mark of the church's truth. If the church's task is to stimulate holiness at close quarters, it cannot militate against her character as holy that she has false members clinging to her truth and hypocrites in her midst. Whenever the church retains unworthy members in her midst, she hopes for their amendment.

A leading confirmation of the church's holiness, ironically, is that the church is found amidst sinners—redeeming, reaching out, healing, and sanctifying. That sinners especially resort to the church in evil times is an empirical evidence of its proximate holiness.

The church is holy because her Lord is holy, and her task is to fashion her members after her Lord. The most radical form of divine holiness is that personal form which becomes incarnate within the history of sin to die on the cross. God does not evidence holiness by maintaining a cautious distance away from the history of sin, but by engaging and transforming it.

Since the Christian community remains salt, light, and leaven within the world, it cannot disentangle itself wholly from the world without removing itself from the very arena of its apostolic mission. It purifies and cleanses its life only by a constant rhythm of infinite distance and intense closeness to the world, gathering for worship and scattering for vocation. The paradox of the church is that it is in but not of the world. This remains a divine mystery that entirely baffles sociological description.

In triage those most desperately fallen are those most urgently sought out and cared for. So it was in Jesus' ministry, as we see in his parable of the lost sheep (Luke 15:4): sinners remain God's foremost concern. In its pursuit of holy living, the church cannot shrewdly limit its ministries to those most likely candidates for sainthood. The church has repeatedly found in the most notorious sinners (from Mary Magdalene and Pharisee Saul of Tarsus to the profligate Augustine and slaver John Newton) its most radiant and winning advocates. The skid row missions have nurtured many saints who would not have been nourished if the church remained aloof from skid row.

It does not take sociological expertise to recognize that there are few sins in the world which are not also found among the baptized. No church I know has yet become purified from lust, nationalism, envy, pride, or racism, and the list goes on. The Bible does not characteristically try to dissemble the sins of the people of God, either publicly or before God. Rather the community of faith is precisely that rare place where people are brought to the specific awareness of the depths of their own sin, in order to receive the convicting and forgiving grace of God. The temple is no place for hollow pretense of righteousness.

The deeper irony is that the evidences of sin that are always found in and around the body of Christ may become indirect intimations of its holiness. It could not be a holy church if it had clean hands, as if severed from its task of saving sinners and healing human hurt.

The very purpose of the church is the transformation of sinners. Hence the paradoxical proximity of sin to the church. The task requires that the reconciling community love at close quarters the sinners it is called to save. The church that pretends to have no taint of sin within its precincts is likely to have misunderstood its mission.

Recently I received communion kneeling between a seeming itinerating saint returned from a long life of rugged missionary service, and a weak, gluttonous yahoo. Wedged in at the communion rail, the luxurious irony of the living body of Christ began to stir in me. The church is being made holy through repentance, which paradoxically emerges precisely in the process of recognizing her own unholiness.

John Chrysostom, who decisively shaped the life of prayer of the eastern church tradition, wrote with great delicacy on how Christ loved the church not so much *because* of her beauty, but *despite* her lack of it, eliciting beauty from her eyes: "For he who loves does not investigate character. Love does not regard uncomeliness. For this reason it is called love because it so often has affection for one who is unattractive. So did Christ. He saw one who was uncomely—for comely I would not call her—and he loved her. He makes her young" (To Eutropius, NPNF 1 IX, p. 262; cf. Kierkegaard, Works of Love, pp. 153–71).

This is why the holiness of the church is best expressed in

the imperfect tense as unfinished—that God is now sanctifying the church, now calling forth a communion of saints, as in First Peter: "You also, like living stones, *are being built (oikodomeisthe)* into a spiritual house to be a holy priesthood," "a people belonging to God" (1 Pet. 2:4, 9). What most sharply distinguishes this set-apart community when it is most truly being itself is precisely its readiness to recognize its sin in the presence of the merciful Word of divine forgiveness.

The church is being made holy by waiting upon God's holiness which is forever eliciting modest, palpable refractions of divine mercy precisely through unpretentious human relationships. The church is being made holy by attending to God's own timing, so as to allow the seeds of holiness to grow in time. This is why a key evidence of the holiness of the church is patience. The believing community is called to let patience have her perfect work (James 1:4), to run with patience the race that is set (Heb. 12:1), and in patience to possess her soul (Luke 21:19).

As the motto "HOLY TO THE LORD" was stamped on the bells of the horses and cooking pots in ancient Israel (Zech. 14:20), so this holiness is being stamped on every button or sandal, every discrete action and fragrance of the confessing church. There is a kind of sanctity credited mercifully to the believing church by the atoning gift of the Son on the cross. The whole church is already in some sense sanctified merely by having in faith received the forgiving Word, for "You are *already clean* because of the word I have spoken to you" (John 15:3, italics added). This graciously attributed holiness is not destroyed by the aroma of corruption that pervades the situation to which the proclaiming community is addressing itself, and with which, due to its explicit hands-on mission, it will be rubbing shoulders.

Paul addressed his first letter to Corinth "to those sanctified in Christ Jesus and *called to be holy (kletoi hagioi)*, together with *all those everywhere who call* on the name of our Lord" (1 Cor. 1:2, italics added), who having been made holy by faith in the verdict of divine pardon, are now called

16

practically to walk in the way of holiness, along with others everywhere who pray and hear the Word, however imperfectly. Called by the holy God to holiness, the church calls upon the holy God for the grace that enables a proximate refraction of God's holiness under the conditions of sin.

In all this there is no fooling the Lord. For "The Lord knows those who are his," yet this makes it ever more imperative that "Everyone who confesses the name of the Lord must run away from wickedness" (2 Tim. 2:19). This is the two-fold watchword that Paul left with Timothy in his last letter, as if inscribed on the foundation of the church.

It took me a long time to notice how few theologians of our century have given serious attention to the holiness of the church. Brunner argued the church into invisibility, Moltmann into ideology. Reinhold Niebuhr was so fixated upon the sin of the church that he could not glimpse even the slightest sliver of its holiness. Tillich was indifferently bored by the visible church. Whenever Bultmann spoke of the church as an empirical community, it appeared to be a deterioration of the kerygma. Insofar as liberation theology has approached the theme of congregational holiness or ecclesial discipline, it has focussed mainly upon blaming the visible church for racism, poverty, and nationalism. After decades of neglect, the ancient Christian celebration of the holiness of the church begs to be recovered.

# Introduction

# Whatever Became of the Disciplined Community?

The turning point we celebrate today is this: The reconciling community has in fact outlived the dissolution of modernity. It is a fact: Evangelical spirituality, scholarship, preaching, pastoral care, and institutional life have against all odds already weathered most of the waning winter of modernity.

## The Post-modern Recovery of Confessional Discipline

We are witnessing an emerging resolve in worldwide Christian orthodoxy to renew familiar, classic spiritual disciplines: daily Scripture reading, prayer, mutual care of souls, and intensive primary group accountability. On the same recovery list is the special focus of this study: ongoing, personal, honest confession of sin.

Having been disillusioned by the illusions of modernity, the faithful are now engaged in a low-keyed, quiet determination unpretentiously to return to the spiritual disciplines that have profoundly shaped our history and common life together, and in fact enabled our survival.

The longest mislaid and most urgently needed spiritual discipline to be recovered is godly repentance. My vocation is to reground this teaching in Scripture and classic Christian wisdom. Amid any cultural death, gracious gifts of providential guidance are being proffered to human imagination, along with precipitous risks. Human folly and sin are being curbed by the quiet hedging action of God in history.

Those made alive by the Spirit, whose lives are hid in Christ, enter the post-modern ethos confidently. Those enlivened by the reemergent vitality of classic Christian forms of pastoral care, preaching, worship, and spiritual formation are now living and breathing in a refreshing atmosphere, in a fecund, volatile, potentially pivotal period of apostolic opportunity and consequential witness. Long-set-aside possibilities and aptitudes for spiritual deep-diving are at long last viable which have had a history of being repeatedly disdained by modernity. We need not be driven to despair by the pressures postmodern possibilities thrust upon us. They offer the witnessing community an unparalleled opportunity.

What makes this postmodern grace-empowered discipline *"post"* is the fact that it is no longer intimidated by modernity. Many pilgrims in evangelical spirituality have doubly paid their dues to modernity, and now search for forgotten wisdoms long ruled out by the narrowly fixated dogmas of enlightenment, empiricism, and idealism.

This does not prevent the faithful from appreciating the technological, economic and social achievements of modernity. This can be done precisely while soberly recognizing that the ideological underpinnings of modernity now face radical crisis.

## A Gentle Caveat on the Misapplication of the Term "Post-Modern"

All I mean by *post-modern* is the course of actual history following the death of modernity. By *modernity* I mean the period, the ideology, and the malaise of the time from 1789 to 1989, from the Bastille to the Berlin Wall.

I have learned, when avant garde academics bandy about the term "postmodern," that it is usually more accurate to strike *post* and insert *ultra* . For guild scholars, postmodern typically means simply hypermodern, where the value assumptions of modernity are nostalgically recollected, and ancient wisdoms compulsively disparaged. Meanwhile the emergent actual postmodernity that is being suffered through outside the ivory tower has not yet been rightly appraised by those in it.

Postmodern consciousness is better defined by Christian believers simply as that form of consciousness that necessarily must follow the era of spent modernity (the *period* from 1789 to 1989 which characteristically embraced an enlightenment *worldview* now in grave *malaise*). If one takes the premise that the modernity I am describing is lurching toward death, and that history will continue, whatever it is that will continue will be postmodernity. If X is ending, then post-X is emerging. If what is ending is rightly named modernity, then what is to follow its death we call postmodernity. This is less an ideological program than a simple succession. "Post" is the Latin prefix meaning after, following upon, later than. So postmodernity in my meaning is nothing more or less enigmatic than *what follows modernity.*

What follows is another cycle of inquiry into post-modern classical Christian consciousness, a theme I have previously charted in *Agenda for Theology, After Modernity. . . What?;* *Two Worlds: Notes on the Death of Modernity in America and Russia;* and *Requiem: A Lament in Three Movements,* yet applied now for the first time deliberately to the questions of confession, discipline, admonition, and the governance of the church.

# The Joyful Return

What is happening today is a profound rediscovery of the texts and wisdom of the long-neglected patristic pastoral tradition. For many evangelicals this means especially the eastern church fathers of the first five Christian centuries.

What is happening amid this historical situation is a joyous return to the sacred texts of Christian Scripture and the consensual exegetical guides of the formative period of scriptural interpretation. Postmodern disciples are those who, having entered in good faith into the disciplines of modernity, and having become disillusioned with the illusions of modernity, are again studying the word of God made known in history as attested by prophetic and apostolic witnesses whose testimonies have become perennial texts for this worldwide, multicultural, multigenerational remembering and celebrating and reconciling community of pardon.

There was a time when I (a former Marxist-Freudian-Bultmannian deconstructionist) distrusted anything that faintly smelled of orthodoxy. Now I relish poring over the abundant diversity of orthodox Scripture interpretation. I happily embrace the term paleo-orthodox if for no other reason than to signal clearly that I do not mean a once-fashionable neo-orthodoxy.

We are today experiencing a refreshing breeze of classic theological liberation. The emergent paleo-orthodoxy understands itself to be postcritical, postliberationist, postmodern, post-fundamentalist, post-neo-anything since the further one "progresses" from ancient apostolic testimony the less hopeful becomes the human condition.

Liberal Christianity has lived through a desperate game—the attempt to find some modern ideology, methodology, psychology, philosophy, or sociology that could conveniently substitute for apostolic teaching. That game is all over. We now have no choice but to think about modernity amid the collapse of modernity. We must reassess the role of psychoanalysis amid the disintegration of psychoanalysis. We must appraise secularization amid the impending interior moral collapse of secularizing relativism.

I do not despair over modernity. I do celebrate the providence of God that works amid all cultures—premodern, modern, and postmodern personal histories. Most people I know are already living in a postmodern situation, though they may still worship the gods of modernity which everyday are being found to have clay feet.

As a son of the liberal tradition, before I learned to live theologically out of the ancient Christian writers, I had been steadily asking questions on the hidden premise of four key value assumptions of modern consciousness: hedonic self-actualization, autonomous individualism, reductive naturalism, and absolute moral relativism. Now my questions are being shaped by ancient consensual classic Christian wrestlings with holy writ. Then I was using the biblical text instrumentally, sporadically, and eisegetically to support previously held modern ideological commitments. Now the Bible is asking my questions more deeply than I ever could. Then I was mildly contemptuous of patristic exegesis; now I thrive daily on the testimony of the earliest Christian commentators on Hebrew Scripture and the New Testament.

It was while reading Vincent of Lerins' fifth-century aids to remembering (*Commonitory*) that I gained the essential hermeneutical foothold in defining generally received ecumenical teaching under the threefold test of catholicity as "that which has been believed everywhere, always, and by all" (*quod ubique, quod semper, quod ab omnibus creditum est,* Commonitory, 2). From then on it was a straightforward matter of searching modestly to identify those shared teachings.

# The Embedding
# of Classic Christian References

I do not assume that my reader already embraces classic ecumenical teachings of East or West on repentance, admonition, confession, and discipline. I ask only that a fair hearing be given to the ways in which ancient Christian teaching reasoned about its own ways of corrective love. I will neither evade nor eviscerate the traditional language of the disciplined community, nor seek constantly to substitute diluted terms congenial to modern ears.

The tested language of the ancient church speaks in its own unrelenting ways to modern minds struggling with the follies and limits of modern consciousness. References to classic texts are embedded in all my sentences in order to encourage others to pursue them and become more aware of the textual pit from which Christian teaching of God's own tough love is still being digged. Deteriorating modern ideologies must now catch up with the ever new forgings of classic Christianity, not the other way around.

I make only one pledge to you: to focus singlemindedly upon classic consensual assent to apostolic teaching regarding confession, admonition, and discipline. Without denying the cultural varieties of that assent, this means that I will be exploring long-deferred once-embarrassing questions on apostasy, heresy, the power of the keys, excommunication, communion discipline, and the pastoral care of those lapsed into idolatry. I am pledged not to become spellbound by the ever-spawning species of current critical psychological or sociological opinion, but instead to be a vessel for the reappropriation of the classic texts themselves.

The weighting of these embedded references may be compared to a pyramid of sources with Scripture as the foundational base on which then the early Christian writers built—first pre-Nicene then post-Nicene, as the supporting mass or trunk, then the best of medieval followed by leading Reformation writers at the narrowing center, and more recent interpreters at the smaller, tapering apex, but only those who grasp and express the anteceding mind of the believing historic church. I am pledged not to try heroically to turn that pyramid upside down, as have those guild theologians who most value only what is most recent.

I cite earlier rather than later sources not because older is sentimentally fawned upon, but because they have had longer to shape historic Christian consensus. Consent-expressing exegetes are referenced more frequently than those whose work is characterized by individual creativity, controversial brilliance, stunning rhetoric, or speculative genius.

Who are the "principal consensual exegetes" to whom irenic, classic pastoral theology so frequently turns for advice on confession? Above all they are the seven leading ecumenical councils received by patristic, medieval, Lutheran, Calvinist, and Anglican consent, supplemented by early synods that came to be decisively quoted as effectively representing the mind of the believing church. Supplementing this conciliar tradition, there are the four leading doctors of the eastern church tradition (Athanasius, Basil, Gregory Nazianzen, John Chrysostom), and of the west (Ambrose, Jerome, Augustine, and Gregory the Great), as well as others who have been perennially valued for accurately stating points of general lay consensus on confessional practice: Cyril of Jerusalem, Cyril of Alexandria, Hilary, Leo, John of Damascus, Thomas Aquinas, Luther, and Calvin. "Classic" in this definition includes classic Reformation sources from Luther, Melanchthon, and Calvin, through Chemnitz and Hollaz to Wesley and Edwards, and consensus-bearing Protestant formularies consistent with ancient consensual exegesis. While many differences of opinion exist within the great culturally-variable arena of that milieu of classical Christianity, our focus is not on differences but on textual evidence of layers of shared consent. These evidences we will set forth textually in what follows.

# How I Escaped the Secularist Guilt Factory

Guilt-buttons that once could turn on a frenzy of WASP-liberal remorse now no longer connect. I am less vulnerable to the secularist guilt industry than I once was. The modern guilt factory played a key role in gradually educating me out of modernity.

My penitential assignment is not to confess someone else's sin but my own. I can either choose to collude with mass media guilt manipulation or not collude. By grace I am gradually learning to collude less.

It is not bad religion alone that creates neurotic guilt. Secularizing anti-religion also generates its own legalisms and mechanisms of guilt: guilt over tolerance; guilt over convictions that claim to tell the truth; guilt over ecological oversight or neglect; guilt over one's gender; guilt over the profit motive that energizes entrepreneurial job-creation; guilt over long-defunct patriarchalisms; guilt over any resistance given to allowing the life-planners to regulate individual choice.

Liberation theology now stands poised to be profoundly reshaped by classical consensual Christian exegesis and penitential practice. It has provided fuel for the Marxist guilt factory. Now I stand ever more gratefully aware of the extraordinarily varied gifts of pious women, but not on the ground of enlightenment or hyperegalitarian or dated radical feminist premises.

## The Guilt Dance

It takes two to do the guilt dance. Now I am gradually learning to say to secular guilt-elicitors: You may dance this one by yourself. And when some try to make me feel guilty about my history, gender, race, and social location, etc., over which I have minimal voluntary control, I rediscover that I have better things to do than yield to being nagged and censured about choices others made long before I came along. My penitential assignment is not to confess others' sins but my own.

I do not mean to imply that there is no intergenerational transmission of sin, or that there is no intercessory task of the church to pray for the sins of the community or family or nation or economic order. Nor do I mean to neglect the social character of sin, the flow of sin through vast demonic political and economic structures, nor do I wish to withdraw into a privatistic autonomous individualism. All of these points I have elsewhere written about passionately.

What do I mean then? There is a malevolent guilt industry at work overtime in both secularizing ideologies that live in denial of personal guilt, and in religious misunderstandings that never have quite grasped the nature of forgiveness. The Marxist guilt factory wants to make me feel guilty that I belong to an oppressing class. The PC (political correctness) guilt factory wants to make me feel guilty that Columbus discovered America. The Nation of Islam wants to intensify my guilt that my skin is white and that I am the beneficiary of racism. The feminist guilt machine wants to make me feel guilty that I belong to a uniformly oppressing sex.

Each of these instances is arguable, but my point is that the deeper classic Christian understanding of penitence focuses not on what my grandmother involuntarily did, but what I voluntarily am now doing.

Confessing my own sin is hard enough. It is my task, not another's. I do not need to add every day to that burden of legitimate guilt all the misdeeds of all my ancestors and all previous offenders of my gender and all previous racial offenses of my variegated ethnic streams. I can remember with regret that I have been a participant in transgenerational sin (the sins of my great-grandparents, my gender, my race). But if I become so preoccupied with intergenerational sin that I forget or excuse my own, then I have not a contrite heart.

## The Intergenerational Blame Game

None of these guilt machines is entirely in error, for each could appeal to conscience only if it had some element of truth, but they work overtime, and are often less interested in working through to new life, absolution, and reparation, than in making blame-game points. Compulsive blaming is an interpersonal strategy that seeks to relieve guilt by locating it in some other quarter than my own willing.

Christian pre-eucharistic self-examination and confession focus on specific actions, in particular times, with actual people in which I have offended God's holy laws and lied and harmed my neighbor and dishonored God.

The blame game often becomes a rationalization for avoiding my personal guilt. If I am a black woman and recognize these vast intergenerational structures of injustice, and if I allow myself to be tempted by the thought that my suffering is 100 percent (not 99 percent, not 98 percent) due to others' sins, then I have not yet learned to confess my sins and my blaming may become an avoidance of my own inadvertent collusions with intergenerational structures of sin. When I come to confession I do not focus on others' socially determined sin, but my own self-determined sin. God calls me to confess not Columbus' sins, but my own.

Yet if I become so fixated on my own individual sin that I fail to recognize the intergenerational and social aftermath of my sin, and its consequences for other people, harming my children and grandchildren's generation in intricate ripple effects, then I have also failed once again to recognize the depth of my personal sin. My willed sin has the potentiality of harming my associates, my friends, my wife, my children, especially those closest to me, my "next-ones," my neighbors (Augustine, On the Grace of Christ and On Original Sin, NPNF 1 V:237–256; Luther, LW 3:136–139, 32:92-94).

Meanwhile the mercy of God does not allow guilt to be transmitted for more than three or four generations. Human freedom is absurdly capable of ugly defiance of God and persistent harm of the neighbor, and envy and lust; but God will not allow those influences, damaging as they are, to extend beyond the third or fourth generation (Exod. 20:4, 34:7; Num. 14:18; cf. 2 Kings 10:30, 15:12). God's mercy hedges guilt within the time frame of a century, and by that time prevening and convicting and hedging grace has largely washed, by divine grace or pruned by divine judgment, that guilt out of the system of the history of sin.

But might the guilt of a Napoleon on Hitler or Stalin seep or stretch into many centuries? Arguably perhaps in some extreme cases that can be plausible, but in most families the sins of the fathers may lengthen into two or three or at most four generations, but by that time it has been so diluted by subsequent human decisions that only traces of it can be found in the ocean of sin.

Yes, my Irish and Huegenot and Norse and Scottish forebears had checkered histories, like the rest of us. I belong to a pioneer generation that benefitted from the genocide of the Sioux and the Apache and Comanche, but I was not there to make accountable decisions, hence cannot be held volitionally accountable, whereas I am here and my actual decisions are accountable before God and my neighbor.

## Questions Ahead for Investigation

Can the postmodern Christian community rediscover the disciplined life? How are we to develop a disciplined community that grounds and enables steady growth in the Christian life? To do this, it is necessary to unpack practically, exegetically, historically, and systematically the essential features of the classic Christian teaching of confession and discipline. Only on that footing can we proceed rightly to grasp the paleo-orthodox basis for the reform of penitential practice, the optimal reconfiguration of disciplinary governance, and the proximate betterment of the sin-laden political order. That is what lies ahead.

Eleven closely interwoven questions lie ahead in eleven chapters, intertwining through the fabric of this argument:

1. By what authority does corrective love proceed?

2. How did the Spirit's work of gentle *correction* come to be so closely related to the epitome of Christian *celebration*: the eucharistic sacrament of reconciliation?

3. How is the narrow way of repentance in baptism linked with the way of repentance in daily prayer for forgiveness and with public penitence in cases of grave sin?

4. Under what conditions is it fitting to break table fellowship with the recalcitrant impenitent? How is the civil

right to withdraw from voluntary community distinguished from the ecclesial right to withhold the eucharist? On what grounds may the eucharistic community—for the good of the community or the individual—withhold the eucharist from the obdurate sinner?

5. Can the office of confessor be meaningfully redefined in the post-modern context?

6. Can a tough-love ministry be reconstituted without diluting the apostolic tradition?

7. Whose responsibility is it to reform and reclaim the disciplined community through corrective love?

8. How is this forgiving, reconciling community being nurtured by the apostolic tradition through varied seasons of cultural transformation?

9. How are Christ's prophetic, priestly, and governing ministries being embodied in the living body of Christ?

10. How does discipline in the civil order differ from discipline within the redeemed, caring community of faith?

11. By what means is the worshiping community best sustained amid its hazardous transit through political change?

All these questions fall into three related but distinguishable topics: *I. The Keys to God's Dwelling Place; II. The Administration of Discipline; and III. Political Restraint in Eschatological Perspective,* which form the three basic headings of our argument.

# Part One

# The Keys
# to God's Dwelling Place

The power of keys—the authority of discipline—belongs not exclusively to ordained ministry, but first of all to the whole people of God, and only by their consent (by due process of ordination) is it representatively assigned to ordained ministers. This is why the postmodern orthodox reform of the seminaries and of ecumenism is not merely a concern of ordained professionals, but of the whole laity.

# 1

# Judgment and Discipline in God's House

The pivotal text on apostolic discipline is Matt. 18:15–19. It introduces the metaphor of keys to God's dwelling place. Seven questions emerge in its interpretation.

## What "Keys" Open and Close What House?

"Keys" symbolize the owner of a house or a city transferring responsibility to a steward or successor. When the owner of a building gives the keys to an overseer to take responsibility on behalf of the whole family or enterprise, that amounts to a direct transfer of authority and agency. To be given the keys to the household of God is symbolically to be given authority to guide and govern the household in accord with the directives of the householder (Calvin, Inst. 3.4.12–23; J. McKenzie, Authority in the Church).

The "power of the keys" (*potestas clavium*) refers metaphorically to the right to admit or deny entry into the dwelling place of God. It implies a restrained and limited authorization to govern in the house according to the Lord's leading.

As the head of a house turns over the keys to the steward, trusting that the steward will admit guests and exclude thieves according to the owner's guidance, so are the "stewards of the mysteries of God" (1 Cor. 4:1 RSV) given analogous spiritual authority, by which the church is ordered and governed, provided they "do all things in the Church as he has prescribed in his Word" (Second Helvetic Conf., CC, p. 157).

The transfer of keys was similarly viewed in the rabbinic tradition. Rabbis exercised the power of the keys over their local covenant family, the synagogue, by teaching Torah and assessing questions of *halakhah*. By this means they opened (or closed, Matt. 23:13) the doors of access to the commands and promises of God.

The power of the keys is the power "to preach the Gospel, to forgive and retain sins, and to administer and distribute the sacraments" (Augsburg Conf., XXVIII, CC, p. 98). The bearer of the keys has the legitimate power to open the gate of the house or city of God to the truly penitent by offering forgiveness, assuming the readiness of the penitent to abide in this wonderful dwelling place (Westminster Conf., XXX.2, CC, p. 227).

## What is the "Power to Bind and Loose"?

When Peter confessed, "You are the Christ, the Son of the living God" (Matt. 16:16), Jesus' reply decisively shaped all subsequent reflections upon the disciplined community. Church order is largely a *midrash* on the extraordinary text that follows: Jesus replied, according to Matthew's account, that flesh and blood has not revealed this to you, Peter, but your Father in heaven, and that on this rock—this confession—I will build my *ekklēsia, my* called-out people, and furthermore,—"I will give you the keys of the kingdom of heaven; whatever you bind on earth will be bound in heaven, and whatever you loose on earth will be loosed in heaven" (Matt. 16:17–19; cf. Is. 22:22; John 1:42; Eph. 2:20; Rev. 3:7; Early Liturgies, ANF VII, p. 545).

The authority to open the doors of the covenant to the nations was thus given to the church as first guided by Peter, who began to exercise that authority on the Day of Pentecost toward those worldwide Jews gathered in Jerusalem, and later beginning in the house of Cornelius toward the Gentiles (Acts 2, 10:24–48).

The power to loose is the power to offer forgiveness in Christ's name. The power to bind is the power to call to repentance, and thus implicitly to further admonish impenitents who are as yet unready faithfully to receive baptism or holy communion (Cyprian, Letters, LXXIII.7, AEG

III, p. 158).

There is no coercive power whatever in Christian discipline, no authorization to dominate or compel. That would run wholly contrary to the freedom for which Christ sets us free and to the grace by which that freedom is upheld. Confession occurs only by volition, willingly. Only freely offered confession readies one for the Lord's table.

The Johannine tradition stated the same authorization but without the metaphor of keys: On the evening of that first day of the week, when the resurrected Lord was sending the disciples into the world, even "as the Father has sent me," breathing on them said: "Receive the Holy Spirit." It is to the Spirit-empowered community that he said: If you who participate in new life by the Son *forgive the sins of any, they are forgiven them;* if you do not forgive them or mediate to them God's forgiveness, they are not forgiven, remaining distant from God's mercy (John 20:22,23, NRSV, italics added).

It was the faithful reception of the Holy Spirit that readied the apostles for such penitential discernment. The apostles were being offered this gift of discretion (Origen, Matthew, Tome XII.10, p. 523, AEG III, pp. 154-5). So is the ongoing apostolate offered it insofar as they continue to live in the Lord as empowered by the Holy Spirit. The remembering and continuing apostolate is called to share the same forgiveness with sinners everywhere.

This empowerment and authorization occurs by the breath of God the Son. Through Jesus, God was speaking his Word. The apostles sensorily perceived and palpably heard the sensation of his speaking, experienced in his breathing out the breath of his Word, coming upon them, entering into them, empowering them.

Three pairs of vivid metaphors describe this commission: lock/unlock (Matt. 16:19), bind/loose (Matt. 16:19; 18:18), remit/retain (John 20:23). The first two are symbolic ways of referring to the third. They authorize the offering of forgiveness and the withholding of forgiveness. One who remits a debt forgives it, while to retain is to continue it as a debit. The remitted debtor is completely released from any further payment.

# Who Authorizes Remission?

The authority to remit is vested not in the sacred ministry as such, as if detached, but in the Gospel. It is the Word of God that forgives, not our words. The Gospel is that by which the sinner's conscience is loosed from the guilt of sin. Those entrusted with this key, the Gospel, did indeed "bind with the Word when it was not believed; they did loose by the Word when it was believed; thus did they by one Word preach both salvation and damnation" (Robert Barnes, Works, 1573, p. 258), assuming that the choice finally to turn away from grace is the choice to voluntarily settle upon a way to which God has eternally said No.

To loose is to proclaim remission of sins in Jesus' name. By refusing to receive the remission of sins, the unbeliever remains by his own decision bound (Thomas Becon, The Castle of Comfort, Works, vol. 2, Cambridge: 1884, p. 566). One looses or unlocks or remits when one offers "by the preaching of the Gospel the merits of Christ and full pardon to such as have lowly and contrite hearts and do unfeignedly repent them, pronouncing unto the same a sure and undoubted forgiveness of their sins and hope of everlasting salvation" (John Jewel, Apology, Works, vol. 3, Cambridge: 1848, p. 60).

In contrast the scribes and religious experts had filched and "taken away the key of knowledge" (Luke 11:52) and "shut the kingdom of heaven in men's faces" (Matt. 23:13). Peter and the apostles were instead authorized to use the keys as intended: to open up the kingdom. This Peter and the apostles opened first to the Jews, then the Samaritans, and finally to the Gentiles (Acts 2:38ff. 8:14ff. Acts 10–11; 15:7). Peter was the first to exercise this empowerment, which was then extended to the apostolate, and to every eucharistic fellowship, every Lord's table.

The authority to remit/retain sin is not an independent or autonomous entitlement to forgive as if that authority were detachable from the Authorizer. This authority was given by Christ to the whole Church, to whom the great commission is addressed and the gift of the Spirit given (John Jewel, Apology, Works III, p. 365). This authority is exercised normally through ministers duly called and ordained to proclaim the Word and administer the Sacrament, but this is a limitation "of expediency rather than of necessity. It is God who forgives through Christ; it is the Church which proclaims His forgiveness through its ministers" (Stott, Confess Your Sins, 63). Ordained ministry is for the benefit (*bene esse*, well-being) of the church, rather than of its *esse*, (its primordial essence), as that without which the forgiveness of God cannot be.

# What "Gates of Hell" Shall Not Prevail?

The coming reign of God is being viewed under the analogy of a walled city that could be entered only through its gates. The gates of the city excluded the enemies of Israel during the Mosaic covenant. After the resurrection and ascension of our Lord, with the descent of the Spirit, access to the city of God is offered to all who desire from the heart to repent and make Peter's confession: "You are the Christ" (Matt. 16:16–19; John Chrysostom, Hom. on Matt. LIV, NPNF 1 X, pp. 332–8).

No national or racial limitation is applicable. The gates of the city of God's mercy are open to all who repenting have faith.

The gates of hell cannot prevail against the assault of the gates of heaven. Within the gates of this city of God, the powers of evil and death (gates of Hades) will never win (Calvin, Comm. XVI, Harmony, pp. 291–2), even if the particular destiny of a finite community of faith seems temporarily in doubt. The kingdom type referred to had once been the expected Messianic kingdom of Davidic hopes, a kingdom which has effectively come in the ascended Son who formed the *ekklēsia* as his own body by the Spirit (Athanasius, Ag. Arians, IV.34, NPNF 2 IV, p. 446).

## Who May Exercise this Power to Petition?

The power of access to the Son's intercession to the Father (the keys) is offered "if two of you on earth agree about anything you ask for," and "where two or three come together in my name" (Matt. 18:19, 20). Wherever a faithful congregation exists, "there is authority to communicate to penitent and believing individuals the Gospel promise" (Jacobs, SCF, p. 403). "Just as the promise of the Gospel belongs certainly and immediately to the entire Church, so the Keys belong immediately to the entire Church, because the Keys are nothing else than the office whereby this promise is communicated to everyone who desires it" (Schmalkald Articles, 343, Jacobs, SCF, p. 403; cf. Luther, The Keys, LW 40, 325–35).

Jesus' intention was that "the apostles should be endued with this power to petition," and that they were to be Spirit-led persons who were to furnish the gathered community with responsible judgment in cases of dispute or grievance. "When, therefore, any Church rightly interprets these apostolic rules, and rightly applies them to particular cases, it then exercises a discipline which is not only approved, but is also confirmed in heaven by the concurring dispensations of God, who respects his own inspirations in the apostles" (Richard Watson, TI, II, p. 604).

## Do Eternal Consequences Ensue?

In much consensual interpretation, these passages (Matt. 16:18, 18:18; John 20:23) were understood to imply that the excision of impenitents by due process from the church would have eternal consequences for the impenitent, unless one undertook penitent and reparative acts of mercy consonant with genuine repentance and received absolution. Further time for repentance may by grace be offered, but the preaching of repentance can do nothing to guarantee this extension of time, as the rich fool with barns full of grain discovered (Luke 12:13–21).

In withholding forgiveness from the impenitent, (sometimes called the retention of sin), there may be occasions when it becomes even necessary to exclude the flagrant sinner from the table of the Lord (Apost. Const., Canons, ANF VII, p. 501). The promise of Jesus to the church is that in such a case its act is not merely a verbal declaration, but an effective act, insofar as its discernment is shaped by apostolic teaching and life in the Spirit (Cyprian, Letters, FC 51, pp. 32, 43–7, 52–6, 104–5, 240–1).

The essence of the power of the keys is conveyed in Jesus' promise to the disciples that "it will not be you speaking, but the Spirit of your Father speaking through you" (Matt. 10:20), hence "He who listens to you listens to me; he who rejects you rejects me; but he who rejects me rejects him who sent me" (Luke 10:16; cf. John 13:20; Tho. Aq., ST Suppl., Q17, III, pp. 2626–9; Calvin, Inst. 3.4.12–23).

## By What Authority Does Discipline Proceed?

In this way, the apostolate is authorized and commanded to exercise intercessory and disciplinary power within the family of God. The commission to offer God's forgiveness to humanity occurs in the context of personal meeting with the resurrected Lord, and the bestowal of the Spirit (John 20).

The personal relation of the living Lord to the called-out people does not diminish from the first to the second generation, or from the second to the twentieth century. The same Lord is contemporary with each disciple in each new cultural-historical setting (Kierkegaard, TC). The ensuing apostolate is being called to discern, by the guidance of the Spirit and the written word of apostolic teaching, those moments and contexts in which God's forgiving mercy is most appropriately to be offered or withheld due to unreadiness to receive it.

The discipline that belongs to and is required of the church is "part of God's method of ruling His Kingdom on earth. No method could be devised that would be exempt from liability to abuse and its consequent evils; but an overruling Spirit prevents these evils from defeating the divine purpose, and no one can be finally lost except through personal obstinacy insusceptible of cure" (Hall, DT, VIII, p. 213).

"Ezra wept over the disobedience of Jerusalem (Ezra 10:1), Jeremiah over its pride (Jer. 13:17), Jesus over its wilful blindness (Luke 19:41ff.)" (Stott, Confess Your Sins, 85). Likewise when some in the visible church become apostate, we weep as we call for reformation of apostolic discipline.


# Interlude: Case Study for Reflection

## The Mission Organization That Inadvertently Misplaced its Mission

The linear argument I am developing will be dotted occasionally with narrative case studies to help bring this reflection down to practical instances. I am inviting you to try reasonably to apply the biblical and patristic arguments to the puzzle of the situation described. Our first case:

A denominational board of missions has ceased sending preaching missionaries abroad, even though that has been its historic, stated mission. It has become essentially a liberated, grant-making enterprise, especially to ideologically tilted groups with exotic political commitments. For over a century the board has been receiving money mostly in small donations from faithful Christians committed to the world mission of the Gospel. Now the accumulations of that endowment have reached many hundreds of millions of dollars.

Since this endowment is vested in a semi-autonomous

agency, church members and donors cannot effectively call the board to accountability. So there it stands aloof in a distant city, unresponsive to the frustrated petitions of local chapters of women's missionary societies. These chapters are withdrawing their support en masse and are determined to create a new agency that will fulfill the original objective of sending Gospel missionaries wherever most needed.

To which agency should the local church board authorize the sending of support? Why? Should a civil action or class action suit be filed against the bureaucracy to require the board to use the resources for the purposes for which they have been given? How would you reason about the merits of such a case? By what means can a wayward bureaucracy of the church be disciplined? Should civil remedies be pursued? What might constitute effective penitence in the general church, in the laity, in the board itself, and in local missionary societies, in search of meaingful reconciliation?

# Recapitulation

Corrective discipline is intrinsic to the well-being of God's household. The metaphor of the keys to God's dwelling place is central to Jesus' teaching on what the church is called to be. The keys refer to the pardon of God, the welcoming of contrite sinners into the coming reign of God.

Christianity offers the power of God to free sinners from sin, proximately in this life, and ultimately in the life to come, or if rejected, leaves the rejector in self-chosen bondage of the will. The gates of hell shall never finally prevail against this divine Word of grace.

# 2

# Communion Discipline

One does not come into or remain in vital communion with the living Lord without repentance and forgiveness of sin (John Chrysostom, Hom. on the Statues, NPNF 1 IX, pp. 471–2). This turning to God is typified in the grace offered in baptism by which one enters into the family of God.

Yet the sin remitted in baptism may recur after baptism. Hence there is need for discipline in the continued struggle with temptation and newly emerging post-baptismal sin (Cyprian, Treatise III, ANF V, p. 437-47; Ambrose, On Repentance, NPNF 2 X, pp. 339–44).

The limited power that is given to the *ekklēsia* is to announce, convey, transmit, and effectively express God's own forgiveness to the truly penitent, or in the case of continued impenitence, to withhold the word of absolution (Tho. Aq., ST III, Q84, II, pp. 2529–39).

This is the governance to which the church is commissioned by her Lord, as if standing in continuity with Christ's own ministry of governance—offering forgiveness to the penitent and by implication withholding forgiveness from the impenitent (Gregory I, Pas. Care, II.6, ACW 11, pp. 259–67; Pius XII, Mystici Corporis, 37, p. 23). This is commonly called, in reference to Matthew 18:18, the power to offer or withhold, or the power of the keys. In this way the guiding-governing office of Christ is shared by the whole body of Christ, just as Christ's priestly and prophetic offices are shared by the whole apostolate (Luther, LW 40:321ff.; Calvin, Inst. 4.12).

## The Questions Ahead

The perennial questions surrounding communion discipline emerged early in the apostolic tradition, and remain still perplexing to us today. Nine of these issues which have puzzled the believing community in the attempt to administer communion discipline, will be addressed in the subtopics of this chapter:

1. To some it may seem disjunctive or ironic that the Spirit's work of gentle *correction* is so closely embedded in the epitome of Christian *celebration*: the eucharistic sacrament of reconciliation. Why is discipline rightly viewed as a feature of eucharistic teaching? How can these seeming polarities be brought together in practice? (*The Gentle Duty: Compassionate Admonition*)

2. Does admonition have its own distinctive structure within time, and attentiveness to timing? (*Promptness in Admonition*)

3. Should a pastor be admonished who refuses to admonish sin? (*The Duty of Reproof*)

4 . Does it demean the grace of baptism to return to the eucharistic table to ask once again for forgiveness—which has already been once for all received in baptism? (*Is Repentance After Baptism Possible?*)

5. Theologically what occurs efficaciously in the prayer of pardon or the words of the minister in the office of absolution? (*Does Anything Effectively Occur by Grace in the Prayer of Absolution?*)

6. Who can make the judgment implied in communion discipline? (*Whose Judgment Presides in the Bidding/ Forbidding Exercise of the Office of the Keys?*)

7. Does absolution take the form of a petition, a declaration, or an offering? (*Forms of Absolution*)

8. In administering the Sacrament of reconciliation, does the pastor have a duty to admonish sins which are prone to lead to spiritual death, and are the people of God owed absolution as right? (*Do the Laity Have a Right to Absolution?*)

9. Is confession directed to sin or to Christ primarily? (*The Character of Sincere Confession*).

10. Has the Spirit provided the contemporary church a means of intergenerational transmission of disciplinary

authority? (*How Mod Rot Has Impoverished Confession*)

11. Finally, should private confession to a minister of God be recovered? How has it occurred that the regular opportunity for personal confession to God has become so grossly overlooked? How is postmodern faith being given the opportunity to relearn and recover the ancient penitential practice of confession prior to eucharistic celebration? (*How Rigorous Should Discipline Be?*)

## The Gentle Duty: Compassionate Admonition

Admonition which is motivated by grace must proceed by love (John Chrysostom, Hom. on the Statues, NPNF 1 IX, pp. 343–8). "There is much wanting both to discipline and to compassion if one be had without the other." The pastor needs "both compassion justly considerate, and discipline affectionately severe" so that "both wine and oil are applied to his wounds; the wine to make them smart, the oil to soothe . . . to the end that through wine what is festering may be purged, and through oil what is curable may be soothed" (Gregory the Great, BPR, NPNF 2 XII, p. 16).

The quality of mercy is not strained—not pushy, not inquisitorial. "It droppeth gentle as the rain from heaven. It is twice blest," as Shakespeare knew—to the one who gives and the one who receives.

In no case may those who offer God's forgiveness justly indulge resentments or private grudges or antipathies under the guise of church discipline (1 Tim. 5:21). Admonition must be candid and truthful, not truculent or vitriolic or aimed inordinately at casting blame (Luther, Ag. the Spiritual Estate, LW 39, pp. 250–3). Admonition must be offered at the right time, not unseasonably, with empathy and kindly care, not in personal anger (John Cassian, Conferences, NPNF 2 XI, pp. 272, 452–4; Tho. Aq., ST II–II, Q33.7, II, pp. 1338–40). It must be accurately and sincerely expressed, not overstated or emotionally charged or hysteric (John Chrysostom, Baptismal Instructions, ACW 31, pp.

98–101).

Gentle admonition and fair-minded reproof rightly come before any thought is entertained of any withholding act of eucharistic discipline, which is typically viewed as a drastic recourse only when all other efforts have failed (Schmalkald Articles, III.9, Schaff, A History of the Creeds, I, pp. 253–6).

## Promptness in Admonition

Paul's open and prompt admonition to Peter (Gal. 2:11) teaches us neither to delay admonition when needed nor avoid it when required (Ephraim Syrus, Homily on Admonition and Repentance, NPNF 2 XIII, pp. 330–6; Calvin, Inst. 2.7.12–13, 4.12.2).

By neglect of small repairs the whole house may be brought to ruin, wrote John Chrysostom (Hom. on the Statues, NPNF 1 IX, p. 470; cf. Hom. on Eph., VI, NPNF 1 XIII, p. 8). Yet one does not spend every hour of every day repairing the roof. Only when it threatens to leak is it timely.

Sins of ignorance or infirmity are to be admonished in a different way than intentional sins of malice or intention. The assurance of forgiveness is not to be offered carelessly to those whose conscience is seared, but to penitents who come contritely to the table of the Lord.

## Duty of Reproof

The maxim is: "He who does not reclaim others from error shows that he himself has gone astray" (Leo, Letters, XV, NPNF 2 XII, p. 25). Avoidance of admonition seems to be a great virtue amid hypertolerationist moral relativism, but never in the family of God.

Corrective love seeks gently to bring offenses from unconscious to conscious levels of awareness: "For the language of reproof is the key of discovery, because by chiding it discloses the fault of which even he who has committed it is often himself unaware." Hence the pastor must not "shrink timidly from speaking freely the things that are right;" remaining "discreet in keeping silence, profitable in speech; lest he either utter what ought to be suppressed or suppress what he ought to utter" (Gregory the Great, BPR, III.14, NPNF 2 XII, p. 38; cf. III.31–IV, pp. 69–72; Clare of Assisi, Rule, CWS, p. 222).

Only those who take sin seriously take forgiveness seriously. "Brothers, if someone is caught in a sin, you who are spiritual should restore him gently. But watch yourself, or you also may be tempted. Carry each other's burdens, and in this way you will fulfill the law of Christ" (Gal. 6:1–2).

The church is authorized to mediate forgiveness, and to restore into its fellowship those who, having offended, have repented and confessed their sin. Amid a world bludgeoned with guilt, the reconciling community still seeks to embody this forgiving spirit.

# Is Repentance After Baptism Possible?

There is a recurrent notion in the early penitential tradition that only one act of repentance is possible, in reference to this troublesome passage from the Letter to the Hebrews: "*It is impossible for those who have once been enlightened*, who have tasted the heavenly gift, who have shared in the Holy Spirit, who have tasted the goodness of the word of God and the powers of the coming age, *if they fall away, to be brought back to repentance*, because to their loss they are crucifying the Son of God all over again and subjecting him to public disgrace" (Heb. 6:4–6, italics added). The problem is not that the text is enigmatic, but that it speaks all too clearly. How do other passages, read by analogy of faith, illumine this one?

The main metaphor here is tasting—experimentally trying on or testing out or sampling Christian faith as a possible, conceivable life style, but not fully partaking in faith in the dying-rising Lord, the faith of baptism.

The eschatological frame is crucial for understanding this passage. Second Peter sounded a similar note of realism: Those who having "escaped the corruption of the world" become "again entangled in it" are "worse off at the end than they were at the beginning" (2 Pet. 2:20). Amid persecution when the end was expected immediately, there would often have been little room or time for a second repentance after baptism. As the parousia appeared to be delayed, some further thinking was required on apostolic premises that would enable further post-baptismal repentance.

Only judgment remains if one rejects the truth of Christ's death for sin. "If we deliberately keep on sinning after we have received the knowledge of the truth, no sacrifice for sins is left" (Heb. 10:26). No alternative sacrifice is offerable. Does this mean that the believer has only one unrepeatable chance for repentance—baptism?

The Shepherd of Hermas spoke of a second repentance as the special favor of God to believers (Vis., 2.2, 3, AF, pp. 165–7; Mand., 4.4.4, AF, p. 188; Sim. 8.11. AF, pp. 230–1). Hermas was keenly aware that he remained vulnerable to many faults after baptism. The fallible sinner can take refuge in the mercy of God in transgressions subsequent to baptism (Hermas, Sim. 9.31.2, AF, p. 255). Those who turn to God with their whole hearts and respond in faith during the remaining days of their lives will be forgiven (Hermas, Mand., 12.6.2, AF, p. 204; Sim. 9.14.1, AF, p. 244; 9.26.6, AF, p. 252).

More rigorous is the language of Tertullian that God "has stationed in the vestibule a second penitence to open to them that knock; but only once, because it is for the second time; it can never open again, because the last time it opened in vain" (On Repentance, 7, ECF, p. 153; cf. ANF III, p. 663).

The later consensual tradition is more generously expressed by Leo: "The manifold mercy of God so assists men when they fall, that not only by the grace of baptism, but also by the remedy of penitence is the hope of eternal life revived, in order that they who have violated the gifts of the

48

second birth, condemning themselves by their own judgment, may attain to remission" (Letters, CVIII, NPNF 2 XII, p. 80).

The renewing of repentance remains a continuing necessity, so long as sin remains in believers (Homily Ascribed to Clement, ANF VII, p. 519). Paul directed his exhortations to repentance to the whole Christian community and not to unbelievers only (Rom. 12:2; Eph. 4:23–24; cf. Rev. 2:5).

# Does Anything Effectively Occur by Grace in the Prayer of Absolution?

Table fellowship with the risen Lord is more than a didactic act of teaching forgiveness. It is the explicit event and office of actually offering anew to the believer God's forgiveness once for all declared in the cross of Christ. It not only verbally proclaims, but actively extends, conveys, and embodies God's forgiveness—in some traditions manually, by the laying on of hands.

The church through Word and Sacrament tenders this grace to sinners, that we may believe. The worshiping community does not withhold forgiveness from sinners who are truly penitent. In offering forgiveness, the church assumes that there is in the penitent a contrite consciousness of sin, without which there could be no premise upon which to proceed to forgive (John Chrysostom, NPNF 1 IX, 418–25; M. Dudley and G. Rowell, ed., Confession and Absolution, 1963, 181ff.).

The offering of forgiveness is intrinsic to the proclamation of the Gospel. Absolution is administered in the context of the preached word as a crucial expression of the ministry of Word and Sacrament (Tertullian, On Repentance, 7–12, ANF III, pp. 662–6). Forgiveness is declared verbally in preaching the Word, and offered as an embodiment in Sacrament (Chemnitz, MWS; Jenson, The Visible Word). As the grace given in Christ's ministry on the cross is announced in proclamation, so it is enacted in Eucharist.

Absolution completes confession of sin, and joins it with confession of Christ. Having confessed, the faithful are then to "receive absolution or forgiveness *from the confessor as from God*" (Luther, Small Catechism, CC, p. 121, italics added).

# Whose Judgment Presides in the Bidding/Forbidding Exercise of the Office of the Keys?

In offering forgiveness, the church is not arrogating to itself the power to judge whether contrition is genuine or sincere, for that only God can judge. Whatever preliminary judgment the eucharistic minister might have about the sincerity of repentance must always remain a provisional judgment offered up in intercessory prayer to God (E. M. Goulburn, Primitive Church Teaching on the Holy Communion, London, 1912).

In manifesting and embodying Christ's governance through his specific commission to mediate the forgiveness of sin, the worshiping community is acknowledging its own prevailing tendencies to sin, to egocentric perceptions, and to persistent idolatry, and does not unilaterally assume that its own present judgment shaped by finite perceptions is indistinguishable from God's final eternal judgment (Luther, LW 53:116–121).

If a minister of God should grossly err in discerning penitential intent in disciplining a member, the misguided censure has no power to affect one's standing before God or the eternal destiny of the faithful, since the grace of discernment has been obstructed and not received. Such a person would remain alive in Christ, and in the church universal. The doctrine of the keys assumes a final judgment, whereas if the ministry of reconciliation does not err in its judgment, its judgment is ratified in heaven (Luther, LW 41:313–342).

Since forgiveness is offered by God alone, the verbal act of absolution by the representative minister essentially has a declarative and intercessory significance and offertory character (Luther, LW 32:45–52). An unjust excision from a particular community cannot do eternal harm in the relation between God and the truly penitent, even though it may do temporal harm as a proximate act of injustice (William of Occam, Opera Politica, Dialog.; Marcilio of Padua, Defensor pacis, II.6; E. Gilson, History of Christian Philosophy in the Middle Ages, pp. 489–99).

True penitence with faith leads first to baptism, or if after baptism to reaffirmation of baptism in returning to the Lord's table. There is an implicit sequential order here, beginning with contrite faith which readies one for reaffirmation of one's earlier baptism, which then allows for full participation in the Sacrament of the Lord's Supper. Having received the grace of both Sacraments, and having fallen from grace again, the proper route back to the throne of grace is once again genuine penitence and right reception of the means of grace (Schmalkald Articles, III.2, BOC, pp. 302–13; BCP).

The church is bound to make use only of that form of discipline consistent with the church's message of mercy and sense of justice. The administration of discipline has only in view the intent to remove obstacles between God and humanity to reconciliation, and thereby to enable forgiveness within a transgenerational community of abiding accountability (Cyprian, The Lapsed, ACW 25, pp. 25–6; P.D. Butterfield, How to Make Your Confession, London: 1961).

There is ample evidence that penitential absolution is a practice well grounded in the life of the church of the oral tradition before the period of the writing of the New Testament. The tradition Paul received maintained: "Whoever, therefore, eats the bread or drinks the cup of the Lord in an unworthy manner will be answerable for the body and blood of the Lord. Examine yourselves, and only then eat of the bread and drink of the cup. For all who eat and drink without discerning the body, eat and drink judgment against themselves" (1 Cor. 11:27–30 NRSV).

As early as the Didache we find an already well-developed explicit appeal to confess sins in church before praying, and in particular before participating in the weekly Eucharist (cf. 1 Cor. 11:28).

## Forms of Absolution

Three forms of absolution are found with varying energies in different periods of Christian history:

- The *petitionary* absolution which earnestly prays that the penitent will be forgiven (common in the early church with its strong sense of eschatological immediacy);
- *Declaratory* or kerygmatic absolution, in which the church proclaims that the forgiveness of sins has become an event on the cross, and is thus a reliable fact because of the redeeming work of Christ (common in the Reformation tradition, which followed confession with an assurance of pardon); and
- The *personally indicative authoritative* absolution—a ministerial, verbal (and often manual) absolution made effective by grace—which makes a concrete statement to this particular penitent that he or she is forgiven of sins, by saying unambiguously, *"I absolve you,"* addressed to a particular person or persons (common in the western pre-Reformation tradition).

The differences between petitioning, declaring, and personally offering absolution are the differences between asking for God's forgiveness, announcing God's forgiveness, and personally embodying God's forgiveness as an official duty of ordained ministry. Each approach needs something of the other to express the fullness of the act of absolution.

In the 1979 Book of Common Prayer the form of absolution (Rite II) blends elements of all three motifs:

"Almighty God, our heavenly Father, who of his great mercy hath promised forgiveness of sins to all those who with hearty repentance and true faith turn unto him, have mercy upon you, pardon and deliver you from all your sins, confirm and strengthen you in all goodness, and bring you to everlasting life." Thomas Aquinas had argued for the sacramental power of the church to pronounce forgiveness through its duly ordered ministry, so that merely by the pronouncement of absolution itself the grace of penance was *ex opere operato* made effective. The Council of Trent held absolution to be a judicial act of offering grace, not merely declaratory, but the efficient cause of forgiveness.

While Roman liturgical practice has been moving from an obligatory private sacrament of penance to a general service of reconciliation in common worship, and thus moving in a more Protestant direction, Protestants are busy retracking what has been misplaced in the overall loss of ecclesial discipline through the misplacement and absence of private confession. Thus while moving in opposite directions, these two traditions ironically have been moving closer toward one another.

## Do the Laity Have a Right to Absolution?

The believer who truly repents may be said to have a moral *right* to hear personally addressed to him in his name the word of the Lord: "Your sins are forgiven" (Mark 2:5 RSV), and "Go, and do not sin again" (John 8:11 RSV). When Christ knocks on the door of the penitent's heart and is willing to forgive, the church has no license to stand in the way and prevent that word from being audibly spoken, plausibly heard, and personally expressed.

It is a word that is best pronounced precisely amid that delicate moment of the soul's transit in which renewed repentance and faith are seasonable and perceived as contextually possible (Luther, LW 22:516–528; 24:210ff.). Thus the ancient practice of penitence—individual confession of

53

sin with an intention to amend and make reparation—is understandable as a right of the believer which the ordained ministry cannot legitimately deny.

By recovering ancient penitential practice, the church is affirming its faith in the work of the Spirit to give life ever anew to believers who have fallen. "Blessed are those who hunger and thirst for righteousness, for they will be filled" (Matt. 5:6). Confession enables the believer to flee vagueness and to become freshly aware of one's own sin and God's own grace. The faithful are humbled ever anew by the recognition that God can find them serviceable in spite of their sins.

There is no doubt that absolution can be a commonly-received grace in public worship. But it can also be a specific act addressed to a particular penitent. It is not that the act of pardon in common worship is deficient, but rather that the needs of penitents are so highly personal that they require time and delicate articulation for existentially meaningful cleansing.

Both the whole community and each individual within it are called jointly to confession, as Basil beautifully summarized: "When day begins to dawn *all in common* as of one voice and one heart intone the psalm of confession to the Lord, *each one* forming his own expression of repentance (*metanoia*)" (Epistle 207, italics added)—each one, that is, individually and personally, *within* common worship.

Private individual confession two to four times a year is not an implausible objective, seeing that we sin so continually. Advent and Lent are fitting seasons within the cycle of Christian seasonal celebrations to structure private confession firmly into the timely flow of the worshipping communities. Discipleship groups and retreats may also offer a specially apt context in which to restore some aspects of classical Christian penitential practice. Western canon law provided at minimum that confession should occur no less than once a year and at Easter (Fourth Lateran Council, 1215).

Confession is more like medicine than food. The hearty meal is offered in the eucharist. Repentance only helps one hear the invitation to the feast (Luther, LW 11:260–266; 28:

204–206).

When do laity especially hunger for confession? Some during times of personal crisis. Others feel a more regular and patterned need to bring their sins to God and to hear the personal address of the forgiving Word. Some maturing laity want to make confession in order to renew their walk with the Lord and increase their spiritual stamina. If the way of penitence is denied the laity, if unreasonable obstacles are placed in the way, an injustice has been done (Luther, LW 51:97–100; 53:82ff., 116ff.).

# The Character of Sincere Confession

Genuine confession is sincere, honest, straightforward, and unconditional, not ambivalent, vague, or secretly clinging to sin. "As there is no sin so small but it deserves damnation, so there is no sin so great that it can bring damnation upon those who truly repent. Men ought not to content themselves with a general repentance" (Westminster Conf., XV, CC, p. 210).

Confession is used in two complementary ways in the New Testament as
- the confession of sin, and
- the confession of Christ.

"If we say that we have no sin, we deceive ourselves, and the truth is not in us. If we confess our sins, he who is faithful and just will forgive us our sins and cleanse us from all unrighteousness" (1 John 1:8–9 NRSV). Paul taught that "if you *confess* with your mouth, 'Jesus is Lord,' and *believe* in your heart that God raised him from the dead, you will be saved. For it is with your *heart* that you believe and are justified, and it is with your *mouth* that you confess and are saved" (Rom. 10:9–11, italics added).

"If anyone acknowledges that Jesus is the Son of God, God lives in him and he in God" (1 John 4:15). One is hardly prepared to confess Christ who has not confessed one's own sin (Clement of Rome, Corinth, 51, 52, ANF I, p. 19). If one confesses one's own sin without confessing Christ, or confesses Christ without confessing one's own sin, the dual dynamic of confession is lacking.

One who attends common worship without ever thinking about serious confession *of sin to Christ* may have the form of godliness without the power thereof (2 Tim. 3:5). The confession-avoiding church-goer may be missing a distinctive gift of the Spirit that belongs to the life of faith—the freedom to confess personal sin and receive personal pardon (Luther, LW 36:358–360). To live in denial of this gift is to live a crippled Christian life. There is a remedy. This community of faith has 2,000 years of experience in offering pardon to the truly penitent.

If mod-rocked believers had earlier grasped the dynamics of corrective love that prevailed consensually in the apostolic tradition, many of the difficulties we have puzzled over could have been better superintended—even impediments that may seem to us proximately irreformable without a special act of grace (Luther, LW 3:343–346).

# How Mod Rot Has Impoverished Confession

Naturalistic reductionism has invited us to reduce alleged individual sins to social influences for which individuals are not responsible. Narcissistic hedonism has demeaned any talk of sin or confession as ungratifying and dysfunctional. Autonomous individualism has divorced sin from a caring community. Absolute relativism has regarded moral values as so ambiguous that there is no measuring rod against which to assess anything as sin. Thus modernity, which is characterized by the confluence of these four ideological streams, has presumed to do away with confession, and has in fact made confession an embarrassment to the accommodating church of modernity.

How inconvenient it is to the accommodating church to realize that modernity is dead, its vitality spent. Now postmodern consciousness is inviting us to a renewed sense of the need for a reconciling, forgiving community. Post-modern Christian consciousness has lived through this quiet valley of despair, and has now come out of this pit more ready to confess sin and joyfully to receive the forgiving Word.

Within the murky halls where the hegemony of modernity still tardily prevails (journalists, academics, ecclesial bureaucrats, and knowledge elites), there remains a despairing tentativeness about the thought that any act might be either intrinsically right or wrong. This amounts to a morally handicapping condition. It compulsively lacks confidence that anything could be clearly an unequivocal requirement of oneself, or of society, much less of God. Social determinations reign. Motivational ambiguities are impenetrable, psychological influences endless.

Post-Freudian penitents are more likely to say I feel these ambivalences, than I have sinned in your presence, Lord. It is hard to distinguish willed, conscious sin from the maze of unconscious influences and the swirl of anxiety and guilt that flood modern consciousness. The classic Christian approach to confession is highly specific and personal. It occurs when I become aware that I have specifically wronged another and my conscience is troubled until I experience the Lord's forgiveness and hear clearly the word of pardon addressed to me personally (Luther, LW 51:97ff.).

If guilt is a key indicator of psychoanalysis, confession of guilt must be essential to its treatment. Guilt is a familiar phenomenon encountered equally by both minister and therapist. Even if the secular psychotherapist is sometimes outwardly contemptuous or ignorant of the traditions of religious confession and penance, that tradition nonetheless has been for centuries engaging in something very much like the dialogue that occurs in psychotherapy, even that which lacks explicit religious language. Those who practice secular psychotherapy apart from the church often work hard to clarify guilt, understand the dynamics of its development, and seek to bring unconscious guilt into awareness—all processes broadly analogous to Christian pastoral care. But psychotherapists are not usually so bold as to try to deal with guilt in the wider sense of appropriating the forgiveness of God. That is precisely what makes absolution all the more important.

## How Rigorous Should Discipline Be?

During second- and third-century persecutions a distinction arose between two types of confession: *Exhomologesis* (*confessio*) in some cases required *publicly* enrolling as a penitent and doing prescribed penance under the supervision of a bishop, for all to see, in a public confession; whereas in other cases confession, according to Cyprian, was a *private* examination of sin in a confidential setting under the guidance of an elder in the apostolic tradition (On the Lapsed, 28; cf. Cyprian, Letter 4).

The unconventional Montanists practiced hyper-rigorist ecclesial discipline on the extreme assumption that the church is actually within history a purified and holy community not solely by grace but in actual behavioral practice. What they feared worst was that the offering of forgiveness might encourage sin. When Tertullian became a Montanist, he placed rigorous limits on second repentance and argued that some sins were forever unforgivable, such as idolatry, murder and adultery.

Cyprian later wrote a corrective treatise on those who had lapsed into idolatry during persecution. He sought to make a way for the truly penitent to be readmitted. Irenaeus, Clement of Alexandria, and Origen all struggled with the question of whether repentance is repeatable (R. C. Mortimer, The Origins of Private Penance in the Western Church, Oxford: Clarendon, 1939, ch. 2; K. Rahner, Penance in the Early Church Theological Investigations, 15; Hyde, DGF 11).

In the persecuted church no more than one absolution was ordinarily permitted. After the Constantinian settlement, there came to be unlimited opportunities, on the premise that divine forgiveness is offered seventy times seven times. Though penitential sentences were often severe (many years), Basil thought a penance well done could be halved in time. "Those who do penance with greater labor quickly obtain the mercy of God" (Epistle 217.74). Penance thus became something analogous to another chance at a rigorous catechumate (Origen, Hom. on Ezek. 3.8). The implication is that some continuing pastoral guidance was occurring during the penitential period. In this way *exhomologesis* became an opportunity for rigorous self-examination and renewal of one's baptismal vow (C&A, 48).

A new era of penitential discipline developed some time after the peace of Constantine, when numerous fair-weather worshippers challenged the church's identity and moral integrity by bringing a lot of cultural garbage and indecency into the church. Through conciliar decisions, monastic spiritual directions, penitential letters, and early canon law, procedures were refined by which penitential practice came to be more discreetly administered.

Here is what typically happened: The penitent believer approached the bishop for permission to become a penitent. If admitted, the penitent was enrolled in the order of penitents and excluded from communion. Though penitents could join in services of worship, they were dismissed with the catechumens before the offering of holy communion, often with cropped hair and special clothing such as the goatskin *cilicium*. While they were numbered among the order of penitents, they often abstained from conjugal relations. They voluntarily performed acts of mercy and almsgiving. The time required for penitence was seldom less than forty days and, depending upon the severity of the sin, could be much longer—years. Upon confession, either in public or private, they were reconciled by episcopal blessing and the laying on of hands and readmitted to communion (J.A.T. Gunstone, The Liturgy of Penance, NY: Morehouse-Barlow, 1966, p. 17–24; Hyde DGF, 10–12).

Protestants must not forget that right penitential practice was the major issue that touched off the Reformation. The first of Luther's 95 Theses challenged the institution of deteriorated sacramental penance as practiced in late medieval scholasticism. Far from wishing to abolish confession, Luther wanted to bring it into greater experiential depth and break free from its manipulative temptations and superstitious aspects (Luther, LW 51:97–100; 53:82ff.). Calvin thought private confession, whether to a pastor or fellow believer, was salutary for the quieting of an uneasy conscience and the correction of the sinner, but not to be regarded as necessary for absolution or as a Sacrament instituted by the Lord.

Self-examination before communion was commended by every pastor as pastoral duty of the English church tradition (Hooker, LEP IV). When the minister says "I absolve thee" it is not as personal judge but as public representative of the church offering the forgiveness of Christ to the penitent faithful (Hyde, DGF 23).

# Interlude: A Case of a Tenet Renounced

A minister has been ordained to preach according to a confessional tradition. Later he decides that he cannot preach or affirm a particular aspect of the confession to which he had once solemnly agreed. He has come to believe in an adoptionist Christology, which his confession strictly forbids. Should he resign? Should he have freedom of the pulpit to preach against the confession? Should he be disciplined by the judicatory authorities?

# Recapitulation

The most gentle of all guidance tasks is loving correction. The work of gentle admonition is closely related to the epitome of Christian bonding: the eucharistic sacrament of reconciliation.

Those who having been baptized, yet lapse again into sin,

are upon genuine contrition welcomed back into the family of God. Absolution completes confession of sin, and joins it with confession of Christ.

Three forms of absolution are found with varying energies in different periods of Christian history: petitionary absolution which earnestly prays that the penitent will be forgiven; kerygmatic absolution, in which the church proclaims that the forgiveness of sins is a fact because of the redeeming work of Christ; and personally indicative authoritative absolution which makes a concrete statement that this particular penitent is forgiven of sins, by saying "I absolve you," with specificity. Each of these three types needs the other complementary voices in order to express the fullness of absolution.

The regular opportunity for private confession to God has been lost sight of in the church that has tragically accommodated itself to the naturalistic assumptions of modernity. It is an aspect of the postmodern freedom of faith to relearn and renew the ancient penitential practice of confession as a part of eucharistic celebration.

# 3

# The Narrow Way

If I have repented conclusively in my baptism or in the confirmation of my baptism, why do I ever need to repent again? How is the narrow way of repentance in baptism correlated with the way of repentance in daily prayer for pardon ("forgive us our trespasses"), and from public penitence in cases of grave sin? How are grave sins which lead to death admonished differently than lighter sins which do not inevitably tend toward death? Should confidential confession to a minister be retained? To whom has the "key of binding" been intergenerationally transmitted?

## The Narrow Way: *Metanoia*

The narrow way to salvation begins with contrition: "Godly sorrow brings repentance that leads to salvation" (2 Cor. 7:10). Narrow (compressed, *thlibō*) is the way that leads to life (Matt. 7:14; Clement of Rome, Corinth 7:1–8.5; Kierkegaard, Christian Discourses). Repentance remains a pivotal Christian doctrine "to be preached by every minister" (Westminster Conf., XV, CC, p. 209). From the outset it has been regarded among "the elementary teachings about Christ" (Heb. 6:1).

The English word "repentance" does not adequately freight the full meaning of reformation of character. It is a less powerful term than the Greek *metanoia*, which implies comprehensive behavioral change (Matt. 3:8; Acts 26:20; Heb. 6:1, 6; Tertullian, On Repentance, ANF III, pp. 657-66; Calvin, Inst. 3.3.5). *Metanoia* denotes a radical change of heart and mind followed by a moral and behavioral reformation of a sinful life, a sorrowing for sin so as to forsake sin and turn away from it. This change of heart, like the vow of matrimony and ordination, has the intent of irrevocability.

True contrition cannot be feigned. Nor can it lack the intent to forsake sin altogether. Genuine repentance occurs only when one earnestly calls to mind one's own misdeeds so as to elicit profound sorrow for sin so as to renounce and forsake all sin (J. Fletcher, Works, III, pp. 112–131; R. Watson, TI II, ch. 19; W. Tillett, PS, pp. 155–174).

Repentance is a fundamental "coming to oneself" (Luke 15:10), a voluntary change of mind, heart, and will in turning away from sin (Clement of Alexandria, Who is the Rich Man That Shall Be Saved?, XXXIX, ANF II, p. 602). "By repentance I mean conviction of sin, producing real desires and sincere resolutions of amendment" (Wesley, WJWB Sermon 7, WJW V, p. 76; A.A. Hodge, OOT, pp. 487–495). Repentance assumes a full commitment of heart and mind to the mortification of those sins that so easily beset us, and to the Spirit's vivification of a new life (Calvin, Inst. 3.3.8).

# The Radical Reversal of Mind, Heart, and Will

Five landmarks of the way of repentance were set forth by John Chrysostom: openly declaring one's sins, forgiving the sins of others indebted to us, diligent prayer, acts of loving-kindness, and unfeigned humility as in the case of the publican (Resisting the Temptations of the Devil, NPNF 1 IX, p. 190).

Evangelical repentance is that repentance required by the Gospel, a godly sorrow elicited in the heart by the Holy Spirit, by which the sinner becomes intensely aware of sin as an offense to divine holiness, and loathes sin's power. One becomes keenly aware of the burden and skewed power of one's own freedom. One turns away from sin in grief over the misdeeds done, and toward God seeking pardon (John Chrysostom, Baptismal Instructions, ACW 31, pp. 50–3; Wesley, WJWB Sermon 9). Evangelical repentance embraces these dimensions of spiritual and moral reversal: conviction of sin, godly sorrow, heartfelt contrition for sin, resolution to forsake all sin, confession (*exhomologesis* to God and where pertinent to offended persons), and moral reformation, including amendment of life and acts of reparation (Homily Ascribed to Clement 13.11; 8.3,4; Tertullian, On Repentance, 9–12, ANF III, pp. 664–666; Irish Articles, 38, COC III, p. 534).

The reversal does not occur without first a *change of mind*, a revised awareness of oneself, utilizing one's own best moral reasoning to recognize the intolerable cost of sin. Where the reversal touches the mind, but not the heart and will, the despair of sin deepens.

Repentance requires a *change of heart*, a deep sorrowing for sin (Ps. 51:4). It is a grieving over one's alienated self and broken relationships, a loathing of sin, and godly sorrow for irresponsibility, a heavy feeling of condemnation which intends to have a constructive effect by changing character and habituation (Rom. 7; Second Clement 9.8; Wesley, WJWB, I, Serm. 9; WJW V, pp. 98–111).

Repentance elicits a *change of will*, a redirected disposition to seek a new life of forgiveness and grateful responsibility. It is a grace-enabled act of willing, a determination to turn the whole self around. Having grieved over his sin, David asked: "Grant me a willing spirit, to sustain me" (Ps. 51:12; Luther, LW 12, pp. 382–4). The inward feeling of remorse moves toward outward behavioral acts which turn away from the life of sin (Apost. Const., II.22–24, ANF VII, p. 406–8).

Conviction of sin came upon Isaiah in the temple filled with smoke:

> "Woe to me!" I cried. "I am ruined! For I am a man of unclean lips, and I live among a people of unclean lips, and my eyes have seen the King, the LORD Almighty." Then one of the seraphs flew to me with a live coal in his hand, which he had taken with tongs from the altar. With it he touched my mouth and said, "See, this has touched your lips; your guilt is taken away and your sin atoned for." (Is.6:5–7)

# Prayer for Reconciliation in 1 John 5:16–17

"If you see your brother or sister committing what is not a mortal sin, *you will ask, and God will give life* to such a one—to those whose sin is not mortal. There is a sin that is mortal; I do not say that you should pray about that. All wrongdoing is sin, but there is sin which is not mortal" (1 John 5:16–17 NRSV, italics added).

The assumption here is that we are actively commanded to pray for a believer's forgiveness when he has fallen. This assumes some knowledge of the believer's sin and evidence of repentance. This suggests that there was a practice operative in which sins against a brother were being openly confessed, either publicly or in the presence of the offended party. When I pray for your sins and thereby effectively participate in your coming to forgiveness, that is no diminution of the importance of the atoning work of Christ, but rather an expression of its importance to the cohesion of the community. The particularly grave sin which the author of 1 John has in mind is false teaching that tends toward apostasy (1 John 2:18–27, 4:1–6). As with Hebrews and Luke, in 1 John, apostasy voluntarily cuts off all avenues to redemption.

"We cannot be sure how the ministry of forgiving and retaining sins was realized in the Johannine church, but it seems more likely that, as in Matthew's church and in Qumran and in the synagogue before them, it was essentially a matter of excommunication and restoration, administered by leaders accredited, by whatever means of elective succession, with the same authority as the apostles" (C&A, 23–4).

The unforgivable "sin against the Spirit" is the refusal of repentance which excludes all possibility of forgiveness. It is to deny Christ by apostasy from the church, which is seen as unpardonable in traditions as varied as Luke, Hebrews, and 1 John.

# Whether Grave Sins Which Lead to Death Are Admonished Differently Than Lighter Sins Which Do Not Inevitably Tend toward Death

The Johannine epistle distinguished between sins that do

"not lead to death", and "sin that leads to death" (1 John 5:16–17; cf. 1 John 2:1; 3:4; Heb. 10:26; Exod. 23:21). This distinction is not a medieval invention. Although the distinction in 1 John between graver and lighter sins cannot be simply translated as mortal and venial, there are many evidences in the earliest Pauline and Johannine traditions that some sins required severance from the eucharistic community—especially apostasy. For they deprive the person of baptismal grace (K. Rahner, Theol. Invest. XV:23ff., 129ff; C&A:44). These capital sins required a *poenitentia major* greater than daily prayer for grace, and this penitence typically required temporary separation from eucharistic gifts.

By the time of Tertullian a functional distinction in disciplinary practice was being made between "sins of daily occurrence" (as forms of anger, cursing, deceptive talk, and backbiting that are not so seated and reinforced as to be unamendable), as distinguished from more serious syndromes of sin that if unrepented lead to spiritual death. This distinction between light sins (*peccata levia*, correctible, less consequential), and grave sins (*peccata gravia*, heinous and less correctible) was argued by Augustine on the basis of 1 Cor. 7:5–6 and 6:1–7 (Augustine, Enchiridion, 78, NPNF 1 III, p. 263).

In the synagogue and Qumran a distinction was made between deliberate and inadvertent sin. The distinction may refer more to motive than gravity. It is based on the Levitical distinction between "sins of the high hand" for which punishment was severe, and "unwitting sins" for which punishment might be remitted (Lev. 4:2ff; Num 15:22–31).

The latter (sometimes called venial, from Lat.: *venia*, grace, kindness) pardonable, excusable sins (that "do not lead to death") do not imply the complete forfeiture of justification and do not require excision from the eucharist (Trent, VI, SCD 804, p. 253), but are forgiven by Christ upon contrite prayer, confession, and works that showed evidence of the fruits of repentance (Trent, XIV.5, pp. 92–4; SCD 899, p. 275).

Grave sins are those which by "gratifying the cravings of our sinful nature," lead to death, so that "In our natural condition we, like the rest, lay under the dreadful judgment of God" (Eph. 2:3 NEB). One who sins mortally has handed himself over as a servant of sin. Justification may be squandered or clouded or misplaced if one again becomes captive habitually to the power of sin (Council of Lyons II, 1274, SCD 464, p. 185; Trent, SCD 808, p. 256; SCD 894–899, pp. 272–275). The mortal or deadly sins are those by which God is always offended and which, unless remitted by forgiveness, make one a deserter, betrayer, and enemy of God (Council of Constance, SCD 628, p. 212; 1290, 3018). Some sin which seems light to the sinner may be made more grave by the force of habit (Augustine, Enchiridion, 78–80, NPNF 1 III, pp. 263–4).

Often counted by ancient Christian writers as among capital or mortal sins were homicide, idolatry, blasphemy, adultery, fornication, fraud (Tertullian, On Modesty, 19, ANF IV. pp. 95–7; cf. Ag. Marcion, IV.9, ANF III, p. 356; cf. Augsburg Apology, Art. XI, BOC, pp. 180–2), which may if left unrepentant require temporary disciplinary excision from the eucharistic community, but upon contrite confession in the presence of the congregation even these could be readmitted to communion in a second repentance after baptism (Tertullian, On Repentance, 7–12, ANF III, pp. 662–6; Apol. 39, p. 46). Among major controversies of patristic reasoning were those that centered on the possibility of a second repentance after apostasy, fornication, or murder (Basil, Canons, NPNF 2 XIV, pp. 606–11; Gregory of Nyssa, Canons, pp. 511–13; Quasten, Patr. III, pp. 422–3; Tho. Aq., ST Suppl. Q21–28, III, pp. 2640–61; Q62, III, pp. 2793–8).

No one who would defiantly persist in profiting from the evils of an astrology, necromancy, prostitution, brothel-keeping, or teaching of pagan myths could conceivably be ready conscientiously to sit at the Lord's table and receive forgiving grace. Such behaviors *prima facie* are demeaning to the life of faith active in love (Hippolytus, The Apostolic Tradition, ed. Botte, 16, cf. C&A 41).

# Three Gateways of Forgiveness: Baptism, Daily Prayer, and Reconciliation after Public Penitence

In the conclusion of his sermon to catechumens on the creed, Augustine summarized classic Christian penitential teaching: "Within the Church, sins are forgiven in three ways: by baptism, by prayer, and by the greater humility of penance" (FC 27:306). First, baptism is the prototype of all subsequent repentance and faith. Secondly, by praying for forgiving grace, we receive forgiveness. Finally by voluntarily submitting to the order of penitents, willing to undergo excommunication and acts of mortification and reparation, with true repentance we are again admissible into the reconciling community (John Haliburton "'A Godly Discipline': Penance in the Early Church," C&A 40ff.).

"Those sins which He forgives in the first way He forgives only to the baptized. When? When they are being baptized. Sins which are forgiven afterwards to those who pray and repent are forgiven them because they have been baptized. For, how can those who are not yet born say 'our Father'?" (Augustine, FC 27:306).

In the early church baptism was the original sacrament of forgiveness. By the grace of baptism, the believer is offered a newly regenerated life empowered by the Spirit. After baptism it is fitting prior to coming to the eucharistic table to ask forgiveness for intervening sins, with sincere intent toward reparation and behavioral change. By its prayer for pardon the church conveys the forgiving Word to the penitent (Luther, Short Order of Confession, LW 53:116–119).

Does this mean that the believer can never sin after baptism? No, we know ourselves too well. Does it mean that the believer ought never to sin after baptism? That in principle is the wished-for consequence of the full reception of sanctifying grace, but not to be unrealistically conceived. "When you have been baptized, hold to the good life in the commandments of God that you may preserve your baptism up to the very end" (Augustine, The Creed, FC 27:305).

But a clarifying caveat follows: "I do not tell you that you will live here without sin; but they are light sins, which are in practice unavoidable in this life" (Augustine, De symbolo ad catechumenos 7.15; cf. NPNF 2 III:374 amended). In the flesh no believer is afflicted with the absurd requirement ceaselessly "to live here altogether free from sin. Nobody passes this life without committing some lesser or more pardonable sins." (Augustine, The Creed, 7.15, C&A, 42). So "How does the prayer go? 'And forgive us our debts, as we also forgive our debtors'" (Augustine, The Creed, 7.15, FC 27:385). Every day the believer prays this prayer (Matt. 6:12). Only those who are by grace enabled to say "Abba, Father", are prepared to utter this prayer rightly. In sum: "We are once washed or cleansed from sin by baptism, we are daily cleansed from sin by prayer" (Augustine, The Creed 7.15, FC 27:305–6; cf. C&A, 42).

But there are graver sins, like murder, adultery, and apostasy, capital sins which mock the reconciling community and undermine the life of grace, "for which it will be necessary to separate out from the body of Christ" (Augustine, De symbolo ad catechumenos 7.15; C&A 42). In these offenses the change of heart required cannot be quickly or easily feigned, and time is needed for repentance.

So the catechumen is admonished to "not commit those sins that compel your separation from the Body of Christ; God forbid that you should! They whom you see doing penance have committed crimes, either adultery, or some other outrage; that is the reason why they are doing penance. If their sins were slight, daily prayer would be enough to destroy them" (FC 27:305–6). Grave sins require separation from the community of grace if grace for the penitent is to be kept honest (Origen, Homily on the Prodigal Son; cf. Luke 10.4).

The notorious sexual abuser who was excluded from the community in 1 Cor. 5:1–8 was not barred simply out of rancor or pique, but to stimulate repentance. Hope is held out for readmission into the community. Just such a restoration is reported in 2 Cor. 2. Evidences of penitents being expelled and/or readmitted to the congregation upon repentance are found abundantly in the New Testament (Acts. 5:2, 2 Thess. 3:14–15, Titus 3:10–12 and Matthew 18). Paul did not regard any sin, no matter how grave, as outside the scope of pastoral discipline or beyond restoration through repentance (G. Lampe, "Church Discipline and the Epistles to the Corinthians," Christian History and Interpretation, ed. W. R. Farmer, Cambridge: 1967, 354f.).

# Whether Confidential Confession to a Minister Should be Retained

Though confession is primarily addressed to God, the ear of a caring human hearer is helpful in making confession real and accountable (Ps. 32:3–5; 1 John 1:9; Neve, Luth. Sym., p. 215). The Augsburg Confession advised that "private absolution ought to be retained in all the churches" (Art. XI) in order that the smitten conscience might be unburdened and comforted prior to Holy Communion (Art. XII; Schmalkald Articles, 331; Jacobs, SCF, p. 443). Luther continued to commend voluntary private confession (Luther, EA, XXIII, p. 68; XXVIII, pp. 248–50, 308; XXIX, p. 353).

The English Church Order of Holy Communion of 1549 provided for the minister to say: "And if there be any of you whose conscience is troubled and grieved in anything, lacking comfort or counsel, let him come to me, or to some other discreet and learned priest taught in the law of God, and confess and open his sin and grief secretly, that he may receive such ghostly counsel, advice, and comfort that his conscience may be relieved, and that of us, as of the ministers of God and of the church, he may receive comfort and absolution, to the satisfaction of his mind and avoiding of all scruple and doubtfulness."

This language has recurred in the English tradition: "In the case of those who cannot quiet their own consciences previous to receiving the Holy Communion, but require further comfort or counsel, the minister is directed to say, 'Let him come to me, or to some other discreet and learned minister of God's Word, and open his grief, that by the ministry of God's Holy Word he may receive the benefit of Absolution, together with ghostly counsel and advice" (Chronicle of the Convocation of Canterbury, London: 1873, p. 558).

The instruction of the 1979 American Book of Common Prayer is similar: "And if, in your preparation, you need help and counsel, then go and open your grief to a discreet and understanding priest, and confess your sins, that you may receive the benefits of absolution, and spiritual counsel and advice; to the removal of scruple and doubt, the assurance of pardon, and the strengthening of your faith."

Meanwhile Protestants have continued to view with dismay certain abuses of the medieval scholastic teaching of individually heard confession and penance, especially insofar as they seemed to have amounted to a stratagem or subterfuge to make laity inordinately dependent upon clergy (Neve, Luth. Sym., p. 213). Sixteenth-century Protestants found it necessary to seek to protect the penitent from the undue tendency of ministers to investigate hidden sins. They viewed confession as a privilege of the troubled conscience to receive grace and forgiveness, not a snare to make oneself vulnerable to inquisition (Calvin, Inst., 3.4).

It is not possible anyway to enumerate all one's sins without some tendency to self-deception (Augsburg Apology, BOC, pp. 180, 185). As self-deceptive sinners, who among us can be absolutely assured of the completeness of our confession (Thomas Becon, The Castle of Comfort)? Protestants found ample evidence in Scripture for individual confession of sin, but often objected to detailed, private, auricular confession to a priest as direct condition for eucharist.

Auricular confession (that heard by the ear of a priest) is not specifically commanded by scripture. Auricular confession ran the danger of becoming an inadvertent trap for compulsive scrupulosity. Protestants recognized the hazard of trying to distinguish too sharply between mortal and venial sins. The confession of sins is a matter of Christian freedom, not of compulsion or external requirement (Schmalkald Articles, BOC, pp. 306, 311–12; Confession and Absolution, Report of the Fulham Con-ference, 1901–2). "Private confession should not be forced with laws" (Schwabach Articles; Seeberg, SHD II, p. 240).

Particular acts of penitence, such as fasting, may "become a form of participation in a special way in the infinite expiation of Christ." On this premise penitents have been urged to give special meaning to their recollection of the cross "by such good works as *volunteer work* in hospitals, *visiting* the sick, *serving* the young in the Faith, *participating* in community affairs, *meeting obligations* to families, friends, neighbors, parishes, and communities" (Fast III, CMM, p. 129). Yet the warning of Leo the Great remains pertinent: "Woe to the dogmatizing of those whose very fasting is turned to sin. For they condemn the creature's nature to the Creator's injury. . . absolutely nothing that exists is evil, nor is anything in nature included in the actually bad. For the good Creator made all things good" (Leo, Sermons, XLII, NPNF 2 XII, p. 157; cf. Letter to Barnabas, 3; Hermas, Similitudes, V.1, 3).

Classic Anglicans like Cranmer, Ridley, Latimer, Becon, and Tyndale commended secret confession to a minister not as recurrently necessary for absolution but encouraged for relieving a troubled conscience. The Thirteen Articles of 1538 commended private confession as "very useful and highly necessary." The Anglican Prayer Book of 1552 commended closet confession (alone before God) as the ordinary means of preparing for the Lord's Supper. Resort to a "discrete and learned minister of God's Word" was encouraged for those "who by this means cannot quiet his own conscience."

## To Whom Has the "Key of Binding" Been Transmitted?

The "key of binding" in penitential discipline belongs rudimentarily to the whole church, and not to ordered ministry only. However, the whole church acts representatively in penitential discipline through its duly ordered ministry, just as in the case of the proclamation of the Word and administration of the Sacraments. As a pastor cannot rightly exercise discipline apart from calling, authorization by the congregation, and due ecclesial process, so neither can the congregation or judicatory rightly exercise discipline apart from a representative minister (Calvin, Inst. 4.3, 6, 7; 4.9.3–7; J.A. Emerton, "Binding and Loosing— Forgiving and Retaining," JTS 13 1962:325–31).

At Corinth, the right ordering of penitential discipline was not dispersed miscellaneously, but carefully administered under the apostle's specific direction (1 Cor. 5:3–5). Church discipline is not regularly to be exercised on a populist basis by the laity independently of ordered ministry (Calvin, Inst. 4.3). For while the power of the keys belongs to the whole church, and not to the ordered ministry only, the ordered ministry is raised up precisely for the purpose of exercising this constructive disciplinary function commensurable with its ministry of Word and Sacrament (Luther, WA 8.173; EA 31.214–18; J. C. Winslow, Confession and Absolution, London, 1960).

Catholics and Protestants largely agree on the necessity and importance of repentance. That they disagree on whether to identify the act of penance as a sacrament has largely to do with how one defines sacrament, and how texts are interpreted concerning dominical authorization (whether it is the Lord who authorizes). Reformed exegesis has remained generally unconvinced that penance was dominically instituted as a visible sign of invisible grace; hence it is not a sacrament.

The Anglican Catechism of the 1979 Book of Common Prayer classifies the Reconciliation of a Penitent (which may be called Penance) as one of the "other sacramental rites," which implies that it is a "means of grace" yet "not necessary for all persons in the same way that Baptism and the Eucharist are" (BCP 1979, 860). It is "the rite in which those who repent of their sins may confess them to God in the presence of a priest, and receive the assurance of pardon and the grace of absolution" (BCP 1979, 861).

The Roman tradition, as well as some Eastern Orthodox and Anglo-Catholic interpreters, viewed penance as a sacrament administered through confession and absolution of sins by a presbyter in historic apostolic succession. The textual grounding for dominical institution is John 20:22–23: "Receive the Holy Spirit. If you forgive the sins of any, they are forgiven them; if you retain the sins of any, they are retained." (NRSV). On this premise it is argued that Jesus himself instituted the rite of penance as a sacrament when he appeared to his disciples after his resurrection and authorized them to forgive sin (John 20:19–23). While Protestants do not concede that auricular confession is a dominically instituted sacrament, they see the grace of repentance as intrinsic to the reconciled Christian life, and the command to proclaim forgiveness as veritably from the Lord himself (Luther, LW 24:210ff.; 32:32ff., 50ff.).

# Whether the Spirit Has Provided a Means of Intergenerational Transmission of Disciplinary Authority

When Jesus transferred the keys of authority over the household to the apostles, one was chosen by him as chief steward. The keys were given not to Peter personally but to Peter within the framework of his office as apostle, and thus generally to the office of apostolic preaching and discipline that stands in the tradition of Peter and the apostles (Tertullian, Scorpiace, 10–15, ANF III, p. 643–8; Luther, LW 40:321–378).

What Christ bestowed upon Peter, he bestowed upon the whole apostolate through him. Peter was the first preacher of the Gospel, both to the Jews on the day of Pentecost, and to the Gentile world following his vision in the house of Cornelius. "In [Peter] himself the Church was reared." He was the "first to unbar in Christ's baptism, the entrance to the heavenly kingdom, in which kingdom are 'loosed' the sins that were before 'bound'" (Tertullian, On Modesty, XXI, ANF IV, p. 99).

The power to gain entry into this house was apparently committed representatively to Peter and thereby to the apostles collectively, and by them it is being entrusted generation by generation by due process to the benefit of the confessing, reconciling community. The Twelve specifically were authorized to pass on this commission to others whom they prepared to follow them in the Lord's teaching. The Council of Sens (1140 A.D.) rejected the view that "the power of binding and loosing was given to the Apostles only, not to their successors" (SCD 379, p. 151).

Hence the responsibility of admonition and discipline is being given to the church not only in the apostolic age, but in its entire period of active witness from Pentecost to Parousia. The duty of protection, guidance and governance was passed regularly from Peter to the apostles and their successors, from James to the Jewish Christian community, and from Paul to the Gentile church (C&Ab, 15–39).

# The Apostolic Authorization to Mediate Forgiveness

There is little doubt that Jesus intended to delegate his own authority to forgive sins to those who followed him in the apostolic tradition. This is the very authority which had offended the Pharisees. This is a pre-resurrection tradition, not a later addition. Being an apostle (from the Hebrew *shaliach*) is precisely to have and be sent out with this authority (Jerome, Commentary on Galatians, 1:1; K. Rengstorf, Apostolos, TDNT: 407ff.). This discussion does not espouse any particular view of succession within the apostolic tradition, a subject I have dealt with extensively in LS, part III.

Binding and loosing meant for Matthew excluding and readmitting an offender. The serving ministry of the New Israel is patterned after the ordering of the Old Israel, but transmuted radically by the humility of the servant Messiah. In Paul's letters we see how the apostolic authority to forgive or retain sins is exemplified, even in the earliest recorded stages of the church's life. Paul, Timothy, and Titus were all exercising apostolic authority to excommunicate and reconcile sinners, assuming synagogue rules of due process. The authorization to forgive and retain sins is made to churches in which the apostle's authority was already being passed to second and third generations of representative ministers. By the time of Eusebius the laying on of hands at the reconciliation of an excommunicated heretic was already viewed as an ancient custom (Church History, VII.2).

There remains a profoundly humbling strain in confession, since all sinners come before God without worldly credentials. As an example, even the Emperor Theodosius was required to undergo a suitable length of penance under the direction of a presbyter appointed by the bishop (Socrates, History of the Church 5.19.1).

There is no reasonable basis on which to conclude that Jesus did not intend to authorize the apostles to admonish, exercise communion discipline, and offer forgiveness (C. K. Barrett, The Signs of an Apostle, London: 1969, 11–15), or that this authorization was delegated only to the first generation of apostles but not to any other generation of apostolic testimony, as if the practice were intended to have died out in the second generation.

# Interlude: A Case of Confidential Communication

A confidential communication under the seal of confession is threatened to be broken: Morton revealed to his pastor under the seal of confidentiality that he has been for years a small time embezzler, but now is strongly committed to reform. In his view moral reform does not require reporting to civil authorities his misdeeds. As a trusted business advisor and comptroller, Morton has been slowly swindling an elderly client over a period of nine years.

Now he has learned that his client requires expensive medical care and cannot pay for it. He has invested well the funds stolen and is now in a position to help out privately, but not in a way that would risk arrest. His pastor knows that Morton's preference for an act of reparation is to not report the matter to authorities, but to handle it confidentially.

A detective knocks on the pastor's door asking questions about Morton. How should the pastor respond? Can the pastor be evasive about Morton's involvement, or keep silence, or finesse some misunderstanding or deception, or should he reveal the offense to the officer?

# Recapitulation

The way is narrow that leads to life. There is no justification without faith, no faith without godly repentance, which calls for a complete change of mind, heart, and will in turning away from the power of sin to receive the forgiving Word. Sins prone to draw the believer inexorably toward spiritual death are distinguished in pastoral dialogue from those sins which do not inevitably tend toward spiritual death.

There are in classic Christianity three gateways of forgiveness: baptism, prayer, and reconciliation after public penitence. Each phase of the grace of repentance is offered in response to the veritable call of the living Lord and is not to be treated reductionistically as if merely psychologically or sociologically determined.

In the apostolic tradition the Spirit has provided a means of intergenerational transmission of disciplinary authority to the reconciling community. The task of loving discipline is renewed in each generation of Christian experience by reappropriating, safeguarding, and transmitting the apostolic tradition.

# Part Two

# The Administration of Communion Discipline

How can the rudiments of a disciplined community be rediscovered? Whose responsibility is it to reform and reclaim the disciplined community through corrective love? How is eucharist discipline applied? How do those shaped by corrective love live out their lives?

# 4

# On Rending and Mending Table Fellowship

Under what conditions is it fitting to break table fellowship with the recalcitrant impenitent? Is excision a meaningful expression of the holiness of the church? How is the civil right to withdraw from voluntary community distinguished from the ecclesial right to withhold the eucharist? On what grounds may the eucharistic community—for the good of the community or the individual—withhold the eucharist from the obdurate sinner? What constitutes due process for public discipline? Where are the moral limits of discipline? Does the community of faith rightly possess any coercive, external, or worldly power, or is it offered by the Spirit only the persuasive power to invite believers to the feast of divine forgiveness, and in grave cases disallow impenitents?

## On Breaking Fellowship With the Recalcitrant Impenitent—Whether Excision is a Meaningful Expression of the Holiness of the Church

The breaking of fellowship is not a later accretion, but harks back to the oldest written documents in the New Testament—the earliest letters of Paul, where a delicately nuanced ethic of restoration was formulated precisely: "If anyone does not obey our instruction in this letter, take special note of him. Do not associate with him, in order that he may feel ashamed. Yet do not regard him as an enemy, but warn him as a brother" (2 Thess. 3:14–15).

Using "old yeast" as a symbol of impurity, Paul wrote to Corinth: "Don't you know that a little yeast works through the whole batch of dough? Get rid of the old yeast that you may be a new batch without yeast—as you really are." As surely as Passover was followed by the Feast of Unleavened Bread, so should the Corinthians, who had received the sacrifice of "Christ, our Passover lamb," now walk in holiness (1 Cor. 5:6–7). "I am writing you that you must not associate with anyone who calls himself a brother but is sexually immoral or greedy, an idolater or a slanderer, a drunkard or a swindler" (1 Cor. 5:11).

Those under discipline are not to be treated in a superficial way as if prematurely ready for table fellowship with the risen Lord. The risen Lord commended the church of Ephesus for its "perseverance" in seeking doctrinal and moral accountability: "I know that you cannot tolerate wicked men, that you have tested those who claim to be apostles but are not, and have found them false" (Rev. 2:2).

In the earliest Christian centuries, persons were forbidden from eating at the Lord's table with those who had behaviorally dishonored Christian profession even while pretending to honor it in words. Impenitents were held as "heathen and publicans"—as if no longer members of the body, separated from it by their own choice, and treated as if they were catechumens needing further baptismal instruction (Calvin, Inst. 4.12). "These are our orders to you, brothers, in the name of our Lord Jesus Christ: hold aloof from every Christian brother who falls into idle habits, and does not follow the tradition you received from us" (2 Thess. 3:6 NEB; cf. Rom. 16:17). Yet even when such a person is temporarily excised from the community, the door remains open to returning upon evidence of repentance.

Consequently, it may become fitting to "exclude from the communion of the Church wicked men whose wickedness is known," (Augsburg Confession, Art. XXVIII) yet always without duress—strictly by non-violent, benign, persuasive, uncoercive means (Luther, The Keys, LW 40:371–2). Three principles apply in such cases:

1. Excision is not to be rashly employed (Ambrose, Duties, NPNF 2 X, p. 65). Censures should be abstained where the end can be obtained by pastoral admonition and conversation. The civil authorities have no right to intrude (Trent, Session XXV.3, pp. 235–6).

2. Excision is intended as a merciful act toward one who is

incorrigible, hoping for reconciliation, and enacted without civil penalties, and by a caring and fair due process (Tho. Aq., ST Suppl., Q21, III, pp. 2640–3).

3. One separated from the body of Christ does not *irreversibly* lose benefit of the means of grace provided by that union. He simply reverts to wilfully becoming once again a novice Christian as if relearning the meaning of his baptism. Excision is a form of discipline that hopes for restoration yet proceeds by temporarily cutting off cheap grace to elicit repentance (1 Cor. 10:13; Gal. 5:19–21).

# The Moral Meaning and Limits of Discipline: Not By Coercion, But Only By Persuasive Means

Discipline is a part of Christ's ordering of the church, not only for fostering the proximate holiness of the church, but also for the spiritual benefit of the offender (Calvin, Inst. 4.12.5). The Holy Spirit works through discipline. Faith is weakened by inordinate accommodation to the world (Ambrose, Duties, NPNF 2 X, pp. 16–18). Yet an overzealous excommunication of confirmed members from holy communion stands in tension with the educative, redemptive, and sanctifying intent of the Sacrament, the offering of which the representative ministry owes to all who are contrite of heart.

The church has no power but Word and Sacrament, hence no penalties other than the withholding of Word of forgiveness and Sacrament of divine-human reconciliation. The strongest remedy that the community can apply is simply excision from its own society and the withholding of its means of grace in cases of extreme obstinacy and impenitent sin. The only powers of church discipline lie in the realm of persuasion, admonition, and reproof, not coercion (Luther, LW 24:321–324, 37:86ff.).

Persons may be "debarred from the Holy Supper if they lack the capacity profitably to receive it. By this means they are relegated to the first stages of belonging to the

Church"—as if they were again catechumens—"and are now to be treated as under instruction, and as Christian minors," yet the church "must never exclude from the hearing of God's Word, and must always hold itself ready to receive the penitent" (Dorner, SCDoc., IV, p. 368).

The doors of the church are not so wide open that anyone one may enter unhindered on any desire or whim whatever. As the Ethiopian eunuch before his admission was examined by Philip as to whether he believed in Christ with his whole heart, so does the eucharistic ministry seek to enable such a self-examination (Acts 8:26–40). "The officers are charged with the keeping of the doors of the Church, and therefore are in a special manner to make trial of the fitness of such who enter" (Cambridge Platform, XII.1, CC, p. 394). Those who are baptized and confirmed as members of the body voluntarily go through careful self-examination as to whether they are duly prepared to receive the grace of the Eucharist.

The conditions for receiving the grace of repentance are honest self-examination, sorrow for sin, confession, revulsion against sin, the determination to reverse the pattern of sin and obey God, and acts of reparation to those injured by one's sin (East. Orth. Catech., p. 78; Henry Bullinger, Of Repentance and the Causes Thereof).

# The Restorative Intent of Discipline and Excision

The chief purpose of discipline is to *restore those fallen by means of a spirit of gentleness* (Gal. 6:1), so that the life of sin may be laid aside, that persons may in due time be "saved on the day of the Lord" (1 Cor. 5:5).

Like an astringent amid an epidemic, corrective love seeks to *resist the infectious process by which the pollution of one infects another* in the community. Uncensured sin threatens to exert contagious influence (Cyprian, Treatise II, ANF V, pp. 430ff.; Dorner, SCDoc. IV, p. 343). If left unchallenged, sin gains momentum and license to spread into the healthy cells of the community of faith.

Corrective love seeks to *bear testimony against deceptive egocentricity and bring truth to light*. It refuses to collude with deception. Those who "live as children of the light" will "have nothing to do with the fruitless deeds of darkness, but rather expose them. For it is shameful even to mention what the disobedient do in secret. But everything exposed by the light becomes visible" (Eph. 5:8-13). One who "conceals his sins" cannot expect to grow in grace, "but whoever confesses and renounces them finds mercy" (Prov. 28:13).

Corrective love seeks to *preserve order and proximate integrity in the church* by distancing the faithful from the scourge of sin. "In the name of the Lord Jesus Christ, we command you, brothers, to keep away from every brother who is idle and does not live according to the teaching you received from us" (2 Thess. 3:6).

The varied layers of intention of church discipline were succinctly summarized by the Westminster Confession:

- reclaiming offending persons;
- deterring others from similar offenses;
- "purging out of that leaven which might infect the whole lump";
- "vindicating the honor of Christ";
- "preventing the wrath of God, which might justly fall upon the Church, if they should suffer his covenant, and the seals thereof, to be profaned by notorious and obstinate offenders" (XXX.3, CC, p. 227).

## Voluntary Submission to Discipline

Excommunication in the early church was at its deepest level of intentionality a voluntary status earnestly applied for by the penitent who having become keenly aware of his fault presented himself to the bishop or presbyters in hope of reconciliation with the church (Tertullian, De oratione 7).

In some areas there were graded stages of readmission:

heinous offenders who stood weeping at the door of the church; those called hearers who were permitted in the back of the church for portions of the service; those formally and publicly admitted as penitents under penitential discipline; penitents who were allowed to stand like catechumens with the congregation in common worship but dismissed before the eucharist; and finally those readmitted to the eucharist (Basil, Epistle, 199.22).

In other venues, after some part of the period of penance had occurred, the penitent stood outside the door of the church, was summoned by the bishop, examined publicly, and if approved was provisionally restored, only to be then formally led out of the church and ceremonially ostracized by the community, there to remain for a specified time at the end of which he would, upon being visited by the bishop, be ready to be formally received back into the reconciling community (Didascalia Apostolorum II.16.1–2; cf. Hermas, Mandates IV:3, 1–6, IV.1.8). The penitent in Syria stood in the presence of the community who was praying for him, the bishop laid hands upon him, and he was reinstated (Didascalia II.18.1–2, II.20.9).

# Due Process in Public Discipline:
# The Testimony of Impartial Witnesses

The procedure for discipline was clearly defined by Jesus in Matthew's Gospel: "If your brother sins against you, go and show him his fault, just between the two of you. If he listens to you, you have won your brother over. But if he will not listen, take one or two others along, so that 'every matter may be established by the testimony of two or three witnesses.' If he refuses to listen to them, tell it to the church; and if he refuses to listen even to the church, treat him as you would a pagan or a tax collector" (Matt. 18:15–17).

This passage suggests an unfolding process of patient clarification to seek reconciliation and avoid unnecessary conflict, moving gradually:

- First round opportunity: confidential admonition;
- If unresolved, second round: the matter is presented to impartial witnesses;
- If unresolved, third round: tell it to the church;
- If unresolved, fourth round: disassociate.

There must be no public censure until confidential conversations have taken place in a spirit of gentleness. In cases of serious offenses by church leaders, "Those who sin are to be rebuked publicly, so that others may take warning" (1 Tim. 5:20). The levels of discipline proceed from admonition to temporary suspension to censure to excommunication (Westminster Conf., XXX.4, p. 227).

# Distinguishing the Civil Right to Withdraw from Voluntary Community and the Ecclesial Right to Withhold the Eucharist

A careful distinction needs to be made between every member's civil right to withdraw from the fellowship of the church and thus entirely circumvent its accompanying requirements, remedies, and disciplines, as distinguished from the ecclesial right of the community to order itself according to Christ's mission (Luther, LW 23:311–313). The latter at times implies the solemn duty of withholding eucharistic grace from the recalcitrant impenitent.

The church has no external civil power or authority or competence to coerce behavior (Calvin, Inst. 4.11,12). Physical penalties belong exclusively to the court, not the *ekklēsia*. The court is concerned that the sinner receive what is justly due in this life, even if penalizing. The church is called in ordinary circumstances to support the court's justice, but beyond that knows of another justice surpassing this finite sphere—final judgment before God (Luther, LW 28:125–128).

The church remembers the justice of the final judgment of God, who beholds the heart and thus judges more justly and finally than any human judge. This eschatological view is the frame of reference for any admonition attempted within the worshiping community. Even the process of excision is grounded in a desire in due time to save, and if rightly administered it comes from tenderness and sympathy, not wrath lacking mercy or hope. Hence "No Christian should lightly be denied communion" (Leo, Letters, X, NPNF 2 XII, p. 11).

Voluntary associations who admit members on conditional grounds have the legal power to remove them for due cause on specified conditions. In the case of the church, its members have voluntarily entered into a special relationship with the Lord, consecrated themselves to a life hid in Christ's righteousness. They are cared for by Christ, and offered the promise of eternal life by him.

In this context, the church seeks to preserve these members in genuine faith, to protect them from distorted teachings and corrupt practices, and to nurture them in union with Christ. Only in this framework are they voluntarily subject to discipline for doctrinal or moral deficiencies (1 Cor. 5:11; Tit. 3:10). Those who stand in defiant opposition to apostolic teaching already have forfeited the favor of Christ before any excision (Cyril of Alexandria, Letters, 14, FC 76, pp. 73–4; Calvin, Inst. 4.12).

Yet the puritanical desire for a sanitized church can itself lead to abuses, as in the case of the Donatists and other zealots whose ambition to exhibit a purified and holy church caused them to fail to show love and patience and prudence, without which holiness becomes a sad legalism and a compulsive spirit of arrogance (Augustine, NPNF 1 IV; Luther, LW 23:203–205).

## Confession to Whom? Public or Private?

Although confession to oneself and the neighbor are significant and should not be neglected, the act of confession of sin is not addressed primarily to oneself or society or neighbor or therapist or pastor, but is finally made in the presence of God (Calvin, Inst. 3.3–4; Barth, CD, IV/4, pp. 57ff.). Since it is with God-given freedom that one sins, it is necessarily the living God with whom the confessor finally has to deal.

Confession may occur in the presence of a trusted pastor or a Christian brother or sister. But confession even then is more addressed to God than the human hearer. "For that confession is sufficient, which is first offered to God, then also to a priest who serves as an intercessor" (Leo the Great, SCD 145, p. 59). Thus it is commended that each one find another, whether clerical or lay, whose life is shaped by the Spirit, through whom the soul may be unburdened and hear the forgiving word (Luther, Lectures on Genesis 31–37, 1544, LW 6, pp. 297–8; SHD I, p. 158–9).

Since it is before God, genuine repentance is a profoundly inward occurrence, as in the case of the tax collector who "stood at a distance. He would not even look up to heaven, but beat his breast and said, 'God, have mercy on me, a sinner'" (Luke 18:13). Without confession (*exhomologesis*), the power of sin continues to mount (Tertullian, On Repentance, 10–11, ANF III, pp. 664–665; Mark the Ascetic, Letter to Nicolas, Philokalia, I, p. 149).

The confession must be as public or interpersonal as the harm has been (Luke 7:37; 1 Cor. 5:2; 2 Cor. 2:5–7). "The repentance of those whose sins are public should be in public" (Rabanas Maurus, De institutione clericorum, II.30; Council of Rheims II, A.D. 813, DUCC II, p. 436).

Private offenses are dealt with according to the scriptural instructions of Matt. 18:15–17 and James 5:19–20. Public offenses are dealt with according to the guidelines found in 1 Cor. 5:3–5; 1 Thess. 5:14, and 2 Thess. 3:6.

The penitential practices of Irish Christianity were introduced into Scotland and France by Columba and Columbanus in the sixth century, and within a few generations private repentance had become the norm, in the place of public repentance (Columba, DCB I, pp. 602–5; Columbanus, Penitential, MPL 130.209–84; McNiell, HCS). After the Council of Chalons, A.D. 813, penitential books began to appear to give pastors instructions for examining penitents and applying appropriate acts of reparation (SCD 894–6, 1111, 1411–17).

Protestants at one time were confident that their free form of confession was a vast improvement upon Catholic private confession to a priest because it is voluntary, demystified, and not routinized. But amid the acids of modernity it has volunteered itself right out of existence. Demystification has dwindled into desacralization. The escape from routinization has become a convenient cover for the demise of repentance. The postmodern pastor is trying to learn anew to listen to the deeper range of feelings of others, without forgetfulness of the Word of God.

A balanced summary of Reformed teaching of confession was set forth by the Second Helvetic Confession: "But we believe that this sincere confession which is made to God alone, either privately between God and the sinner, or publicly in the Church where the general confession of sin is said, is sufficient. . . Therefore it is necessary that we confess our sins to God our Father, and be reconciled with our neighbor if we have offended him. Concerning this kind of confession, the Apostle James says: 'Confess your sins to one another.' If, however, anyone is overwhelmed by the burden of his sins and by perplexing temptations, and will seek counsel, instruction and comfort privately, either from a minister of the Church, or from any other brother who is instructed in God's law, we do not disapprove; just as we also fully approve of that general and public confession of sins which is usually said in Church" (Ch. XIV, BOC 5.095).

# Whether Confession Should be Addressed Interpersonally to the One Most Harmed

If confession is only made in general in common worship, and never to the actually offended neighbor, it conceals a refusal to take sin seriously. (Eric James, The Double Cure, 17). Among the most distinctive works of the Holy Spirit is convicting sin, and reconciling interpersonal conflicts. Thus when we neglect confession, we are resisting, grieving and quenching the interpersonal work of the Spirit (Luther, LW 36:358–60).

The person who has suffered most from my offense is the one who most needs to hear my honest disclosure of sorrow. Sin is most aptly confessed to the very persons who have been most harmed, and with whom interpersonal forgiveness is therefore most meaningful.

Since all sins against the neighbor or oneself are indirectly sins against God, they all are to be confessed to God. Insofar as the sin has been committed against the neighbor, it should be confessed quietly to the neighbor. Insofar as the sin has brought disgrace to the worshipping community, it should be confessed openly to that community or its representative ministers. One is called to use good prudential and seasonable judgment in asking pardon of and making amends to those one has offended. All this belongs to gently admonishing those who have offended.

The reconciling community is called forth by the Lord as the place where the Spirit is seeking to awaken, restore, amend, and reshape life in Christ. The believer has a right to expect that the confessing community, even when it may possess elements of hypocrisy and naivete, will mediate the forgiving mercy of God (Luther, LW 30:213–216). Even when the church fails to be such a community, that does not decrease the need for it, or the biblical requirement that the church be such a healing community.

Since I of dogged conscience cannot easily forgive myself, I cannot quite conceive that God who is infinitely more holy than I could forgive me, even me. But this is precisely the joy of true evangelical repentance: the discovery that if our own hearts condemn us, God is greater than our hearts (1 John 3:20; Kierkegaard, Christian Discourses). When I specify a particular sin, and say honestly to God, "last Thursday I misrepresented the truth with George," that is when the word of forgiveness becomes especially wonderful to behold.

# Interlude: The Case of the Wayward Seminary

I offer another case study for reflection, in order that these issues can be brought closer to the arena of confessional practice.

A theological school with a strong orientation toward an ethic of inclusiveness has by long tradition offered continuous tenure to professors who have proven their teaching and scholarly competencies to secular university colleagues who care little or nothing for the church's witnessing mission. The purpose of tenure is to protect the faculty from irresponsible charges and to sustain a reasonable measure of answerable academic freedom.

The seminary has been taken over by sexual activists who of late conspicuously resist and demean classic Christian moral teaching. Associated with a major private university, the seminary itself is supported by a enviable endowment. The new trustees vigorously support the faculty. All faculty under current appointment are committed to lesbian advocacy, and all strongly affirm the right of self-professed lesbians to teach ordinands. An exclusionary policy monitored by elaborate social constraints in effect prevents anyone not a prolesbian to teach in or even attend the seminary. A committee of alumni has formed to try to recapture leadership in the seminary and hold it accountable to the apostolic tradition. Trustees have been petitioned. A determined effort is underway to change trustee leadership.

As an alum, you are asked to offer support for legal counsel for this reform effort. How do you reason about what you are called to do? The next time you prepare to receive holy communion, you have this situation profoundly on your mind. Before God, what do you confess? Under what conditions should candidates for ministry be sent to this seminary? Should the bishops and church leaders take aggressive action to reclaim the seminary to its original purpose? Or should the resources that have been invested in library and bricks and institution building for a century be abandoned to recent occupants? Who are those most harmed in this situation? Who is called to confess what to whom?

## Recapitulation

The community of faith has no coercive power, only the persuasive power to invite believers to the feast of divine forgiveness, and in grave cases exclude impenitents. While every communicant has the civil right to withdraw from the community of faith and thus to avoid that corrective judgment which belongs within the circle of faith, the eucharistic community may for the good of the community or the individual withhold the eucharist from the obdurate in hopes of repentance and reconciliation.

The reconciling sacrament is not intended for the recalcitrant impenitent, but the repenting faithful. The disciplinary exclusion of the impenitent from the Lord's table has a restorative intent. Those who are incorrigible bring judgment upon themselves by their impenitence.

# 5

# Practicing the Pastoral Office of Confessor

How does conscience direct the conversation? How is prudential freedom exercised in confession without descending to hypertolerance? How might diversions from genuine confession be averted? Is anyone fit for the ministry of pardon who is impatient with listening to human hurt? What makes a confessor more or less approachable? When is it better to say nothing than something?

## Prudential Freedom

Culturally-shaped matters of indifference (*adiaphora*) need not be treated as if necessary for salvation. Conscience need not be burdened by culture-bound arrangements as if they might be thought requisite to final justification (Augsburg Conf., XV, CC, p. 72). Here the Pauline instruction is that "Those who eat must not despise those who abstain, and those who abstain must not pass judgment on those who eat; for God has welcomed them" (Rom. 14:3 NRSV). The underlying premise is: "Each one should be fully convinced in his own mind" (Rom. 14:5).

Corrective love is to be practiced "in such a way that one does not give offense to another and so that there may be no disorder or unbecoming conduct in the church. However, consciences should not be burdened by contending that such things are necessary for salvation" (Augsburg Conf., XXVIII, CC, p. 103). Not every misdeed needs to be made out as a federal case, much less a matter of final judgment.

The penitent always resides within some specific historical context. The ministry of confession must be given some freedom to experiment with its own forms of dialogue, to test the spirits, to assess emergent resistances, to seek out a fitting mode of pardon within the situation. Pastoral care and preaching are given prudential freedom precisely for the purpose of responding flexibly to changing circumstances.

Confession is not reducible to a set of rules, as is canon law (Luther, LW 11:260–266). It swims in the constantly moving stream of particular relationships. Admonition and corrective love are never abstractable from that flow of personal relationships.

Though mistakes will be made in this continuing dialogical experiment, it is better to allow experiment within the consensually-defined boundaries of orthodox faith than to limit freedom too sharply so as to cram every confession in a box or treat every imaginative ploy as a heresy of the faith once delivered. No unnecessary offense should be given, amid confessional dialogue and experimentation, to those struggling with moral weaknesses or those immature in faith (Tertullian, Prescr. ag. Her., APT, pp. 48–94).

Some order is indispensable to mission. Order requires due authorization and limiting of authority (Clement of Rome, Corinth, 40–59, ANF I, pp. 16–20). Extremes should be avoided, as in too much or too little control or freedom or planning or tolerance. Many moral judgments were left unmade by the apostles, and thereby left to be shaped by the Spirit amid the flowing circumstances of emerging socio-cultural situations (Hooker, LEP, III.3.4, 6.1, 10.1, 7).

The empathy required for confessional practice is analogous to a missionary learning another language to listen and speak truly. If another language group is to hear the Gospel, the missioner must first learn that language. The point is not to insure that the Gospel is reserved for a few particular cultures, but that Christ's name may be heard and celebrated in all languages and his forgiving word received. So within each subculture in which sins are confessed and forgiven.

If speech is necessary for Christian teaching, and if human speech varies with different cultures, the church catholic cannot impose upon all cultures a single mode of penitential language or a once-for-all politically correct way of speaking (Hooker, LEP, III.2.1; III.3.4; III.6.1; III.10.1, 7). Luther quipped that the apostles "did not wait until the whole world came to

Jerusalem and learned Hebrew, but gave various tongues for the Apostles to speak wherever they went" (Luther, German Mass and Order of Service, SCF, p. 408; cf. WML VI, p. 172). Those who confine their ministry of confession to a particular language frame or cultural skeleton have not understood either the variability of human cultures or the great commission.

## Curbing Compulsive Disclosure

The pastor prone to compulsive self-disclosure is not yet ready to become an agent of pardon. The parishioner prone to compulsive self-disclosure is not yet ready for the simplicity of humble confession.

Repentance is not emotive exhibitionism. The ever-extending inclination to outdo all others in examining and confessing my sins is itself a gluttony to be repented.

At some point the very act of confession may itself turn into a demeaning violation of the sanctity and dignity of another's personality or one's own. One may become so fixated upon a particular sin that conscience returns to it repeatedly without ever actually dreaming of changing behavior.

It is fitting that both parties understand the universality of sin, aware that the confessor's life also dysfunctions and needs repentance, forgiveness, and reparation. But when the listening care-giver constantly intrudes upon the confession so as to prove conclusively that he himself is just as bad a sinner as the confessant, a wrong turn has been made, a role reversal has occurred.

If there is any danger that a public act of confession might further harm some third party who might unnecessarily be drawn inadvertently into a sequence of sordid events reported, that itself would constitute an added injustice. Another's reputation might be harmed by my well-intended but inconsiderate confession.

In seeking the good of reparation, one may fall into the

evil of becoming inconsiderate of one who might be hurt by careless disclosures. In the effort to rid himself of guilt, further harm may be piled upon the offended. The pastoral confessor must help the penitent see the potential damage reckless disclosure could do.

In seeking the good of sustained candor, the penitent may fall into the excesses of scrupulosity and verbal diarrhea. The special relationship of empathy that prevails in the trusting relationship may itself become addictive. The pastoral confessor will at times work hard to temper this overdependency.

## Parrying Diversions

Trivialized reassurance may circumvent the actual depth of the confession called for. A sin may be taken too lightly or too gravely, either by confessor or penitent.

Hasty endorsement of the penitent's own preliminary interpretation of his culpability may result in misgauging the actual dynamics of guilt. The overt presenting problem may not be the underlying distress for which confession is most needed. Patience is required to allow the conditions to occur in which the penitent can grasp the contours of personal guilt with greater definition and accurate nuance.

When the pastoral confessor places artificial limits on his time, it may block the rivulet meandering toward a deeper stream of confession. If I have internal barriers which prevent me from listening to the dynamics of guilt, I will become an obstacle to the flow of that current. If I squelch feelings or reassure too hastily, I halt the flow, and block the possibility of a deeper cleansing.

When I as pastor gloss over the real guilt you feel concerning your real sin, the dynamics of that guilt are further intensified. Next time it may be harder for you to enter into that special season and interactive disposition in which deep confession is by grace possible.

If I am unaware of the veiled ways in which I may secretly

desire to punish or censure you in your sin, then I am to that degree not qualified to serve as your confessor. My role is not to castigate, but to bring you to voluntary repentance and readiness for the joy of receiving the forgiveness of God.

Pardon and penitence are closely intertwined: "Let the priest be discreet and cautious, so that he may pour wine and oil into the wounds of the injured person like a skilled physician, diligently inquiring into the circumstances both of the sinner and of the sin, so that he may wisely understand what advice he should give him and what remedy he should apply" (Fourth Lateran Council, CC, p. 59; cf. Tho. Aq., ST Suppl., Q6, III, pp. 2586–91).

## The Approachable Confessor

There has been a shift even in liturgical traditions from private to general confession, partly because of the heavy time demands private confession may require. All that is left of confession is a pathetic record of church attendance at holy communion which ends up tucked away in the church secretary's file on Monday. The interpersonal availability of the pastor is crucial to opening the door for guileless confession.

Confession takes time. It cannot be forced. No confession will occur until one is made ready by the Spirit to confess. One who puts pressure on another to confess may drive the penitent into further stratagems of avoidance. If one probes too aggressively into the heart of the confessant, it may propel him into denial or rationalization. Only when he is ready will he take responsibility for his misdeeds.

Believers may be prevented from coming to the Lord's table or seeking a pastor's confidences when they expect stereotypically that the minister will manifest little more than judgmental attitudes, pharisaism and legalism. Some pastors and counselors know only how to deal with sin and guilt on the superficial level of instant cheap forgiveness which trivializes the confession of actual voluntary self-recognized sin. Christian counsel beggars itself when it allows itself to become so enamored by psychological dynamics or judgmental legalism or theological speculation or cheap grace that it refuses to offer the costly grace of repentance.

Whether the person is nominally religious, hostile to religion, or spiritually well-formed, the pastor is called to take the person where he is, and move incrementally toward whatever deeper levels of consciousness of sin and grace are possible.

The moment of confession is not merely when one hears another pronounce the words: God forgives you, or "in God's name I absolve you." Rather it is that point at which the sinner unfeignedly experiences himself as truly judged and pardoned by God.

Sins that have been completely absolved on one occasion sometimes on other occasions cannot be completely forgotten or set aside. They may continue to have a ripple effect. But it is comforting to realize that they are no longer remembered by God, even if traces remain in human memory.

## Confession as Release

Confession releases in language the secrets of the heart. In the presence of another trusted one, the burden of guilt is brought to awareness and quietly laid before God.

Confession is more than getting something off your chest or catharsis or tension release or spiritual refreshment. It is a renewed meeting with the one from whom new life is being received and to whom life has been once for all committed in baptism (Luther, LW 7:272ff.).

Psalm 32 powerfully describes the transition from despairing guilt to freeing confession: "When I kept silent, my bones wasted away through my groaning all day long." The awareness of guilt did not go away just because he was trying to sleep—the silence had physical effect, a wasting away. "For day and night your hand was heavy upon me; my strength was sapped as in the heat of the summer" (Ps. 32:3, 4). Grace came in the convicting form of heaviness, draining that strength that would resist a healing transformation (cf. Ps. 38:4, 69:20; Prov. 25:20; 1 Pet. 1:6). "Then I acknowledged my sin to you and did not cover up my iniquity. I said, 'I will confess my transgressions to the LORD.'" Confession is contrasted with continuing to "cover up" in God's presence. "And you forgave the guilt of my sin. . . Rejoice in the LORD and be glad, you righteous; sing, all you who are upright in heart!" (Ps. 32:3–11). What the sinner had attempted to cover up now becomes covered by divine forgiveness: "Blessed is he whose transgressions are forgiven, whose sins are covered. Blessed is the man whose sin the Lord does not count against him and in whose spirit is no deceit" (Ps. 32:1–2).

A young mother spoke in this way of what she gained from regular confession: ". . . the great release of tension; I can let go and cut the knot of introspection; helps to sort out true/false guilt; helps to mediate acceptance; in confession, I take responsibility and try to work at what I need to confess; absolution comes as a gift. In the past, I suppose I was not free enough to take on board the responsibility. . . now I want to accept my guilt, my responsibility for who I am" (M. Dudley and G. Rowell, C&A:10).

## Sometimes Just Say Nothing

The confessor can nullify the exquisitely seasonable moment of confession by talking instead of listening. When he sees pedagogy and advice as more important than simple listening, he diverts the stream of confession.

Every experienced pastor knows that what the penitent heart says about itself is much more consequential than well-made truthful sentences that shout from the outside of the inner voice of conscience. No element of confession is more crucial than the discipline of listening. The attentive listener is a chosen agent of divine reconciliation. When the moment for keen listening is offered, take it as an inestimable gift.

One trains the eye of confession most closely on what is hurting. If sin is present it will be aching. Confession begins where the raw anguish of conscience is rubbing against the primordial awareness of God's holiness.

It is fruitless to try to prescribe some content that should constitute a particular act of confession. That content will come from within the ache of conscience with its special contours and history.

A delicate balance is required: keep the penitent tautly close to the point of recognizing sin, and then allow the relief of that pressure to flow through forgiveness. Confession increases this tautness, only to clear the path for its release (Kierkegaard, Sickness Unto Death, Christian Discourses).

The penitent already possesses a pummeled ego. He is already upset with himself. This is what draws him toward confession. The shame of revealing his immaturity or confusion to another may itself elicit new waves of despair and anguish.

Amid increasing recognition of the value of public and private confession, the present momentum is toward some extension of the practice of confession, especially attending to its renewed theological and exegetical undergirding. In both liturgical and free church traditions, this momentum is searching for meaningful correlations with preparation for holy communion.

# Interlude: Eucharist in the Name of the Goddess Sophia

An ordained feminist activist in searching for inclusive language has come across the tradition of Christology which has ascribed to Christ the language of Wisdom or Sophia. This minister then devises a eucharist service in which Sophia, now boldly reified as a goddess, is worshipped, and the eucharist is offered in the name of the goddess Sophia. Should one receive communion? On what grounds?

# Recapitulation

In matters not rightly viewed as necessary for salvation, much room is left for prudential judgment in the ministry of confession. Diversions are averted by keeping to the course of how conscience is directing the conversation. The pastor who does not have time to listen to human hurt is hardly fit for the ministry of pardon. There are times when it is better to say nothing than something.

The laity is praying for a new generation of pastors who can enable and wisely facilitate a ministry of confession. Some young ministers are committing themselves missionally to the distinct vocation of recovering confession in the local congregation.

# 6

# Regrounding Tough-Love Administry

The church is not an anarchy where no one rules, or a pure populist democracy where truth is voted in or out by interest-laden sinners, or an oligarchy where a privileged elite rules. Rather, rightly understood, it is attested as a *koinonia* ruled by the Spirit of the living God, with Christ its Head who works "to prepare God's people for works of service, so that the body of Christ may be built up until we all reach unity in the faith" (Eph. 4:12–13a).

What constitutes apt disciplinary governance? What ways and means are instituted by which course corrections are made in the journey of faith?

I am now asking how decisions have been fittingly and consensually made in the apostolic tradition and how Christ's own corrective love is still seeking to shape the confessing community through the Holy Spirit. Within this particular postmodern crisis, how does the *ekklēsia* order itself practically in a way consistent with the forgiving Word? How democratic can the apostolic tradition afford to be? How is cross-cultural variety encouraged within the one body of Christ?

## *Pneuma* Orders *Ekklēsia*

Jesus promised that the Spirit would lead the church into all truth (John 16:12–26). As new situations and societal challenges arose, fate-laden historical choices were made concerning fit organization and strategy for mission.

The Spirit presides contextually over this developing *oikonomia* of God (Acts 13:1–3; 15:28; 1 Cor. 12:8–11). The administration of the church is the work of the Spirit (Acts 20:28; Eph. 4:3–12), who comes to take the place of the ascended Lord, as Vicar of the Son uniting the body. Where this premise of orderly governance is ignored or neglected, nothing can fill the emptiness left in its place.

The Spirit forms, orders, and configures the community of worship (Acts 2:42; 10:44–46), its preaching (1 Thess. 1:5, 6; 1 Pet. 1:12), prayer (Rom. 8:26–27; Eph. 2:18), music (1 Cor. 14:15; Eph. 5:19), and mission (Acts 1:8). The account given by Luke in Acts is a narrative of the acts of the apostles under the guidance of the Spirit who chooses them (Acts 13:2), sends them (13:4), empowers them to speak (13:9), guards them amid persecution (13:50–52), puts the seal of the Spirit upon their work among the nations (15:8), counsels them (15:28), and hedges their way (16:6–7; Gordon, MS, pp. 135ff; Bancroft, CT, p. 174).

Those who, repenting, trust in Christ's righteousness, are offered the grace of baptism, the privilege of common worship and communing with the risen Lord at his table— visible acts in an actual visible fellowship pointing beyond themselves to the life that is hid in Christ. If Pentecost may be likened to ecclesial birth, it is followed by the gradual nurture of the living body of Christ which grows through an embodied history, under God's own succor and daily tutelage, to be ready for an extended ever-new historical mission (Luther, LW 3:154–157).

By the end of the New Testament period this reconciling community was already being equipped with definite offices, leadership tasks, and explicit organizational procedures for the intergenerational transmission of the apostolic tradition (W. Pannenberg, The Church, pp. 99–116; W. Schmitals, The Office of the Apostle in the Early Church).

There is no reason to assume that every trivial aspect of church order, policy, procedure, strategy, or agenda has to be explicitly found in the sacred text. That would bind the wrists of the living body, whose hands need to be at work in the harvest. Yet where the apostolic text speaks in a way that bestows meaning on questions of organization and administration, the reconciling community has attended it carefully.

# The Corrective Administry
# That Enables Reconciliation

*Administry* is that ongoing service which leads to and prepares for other acts and workings of ministry. Administry is an old English word (from Lat.: *administrare*, to manage as a steward) meaning actions taken *toward ministry*, on behalf of *diakonia*.

To administer something is to do whatever is contextually required to practically enable its service or ministry. To engage in administry is to bring life in Christ into practical embodiment through whatever pragmatic means are then and there available within the range of right reason and good conscience. As a visible community, the church in mission always to some extent requires its own distinctive pattern of administry in fit response to its here and now apostolate.

The church in embodying Christ continues and extends his three-fold office (prophet, priest, and shepherd-king) by preaching the living Word, duly administering his Sacraments, and by counseling and disciplining the faithful. No policy is rightly undertaken in the church which is not in some way upbuilding to life in Christ (Luther, LW 13:151ff., 15:26ff.).

This order and organization flow from the very nature of the *ekklēsia* (Clement of Rome, Corinth, 40-42, ANF I, p. 16; Watson, TI, II, p. 573). It is not a negligible point that the disciples had a treasurer (John 13:29). Responsibility must be taken for administering temporal affairs, judging the fitness of leadership, and presiding in common worship.

# Confessional Continuity amid Historical
# Adaptability—The Vine Grows

The *communio sanctorum* lives and grows as an organic unity, a living body. The pilgrim church in history is constantly adapting, adjusting, and responding, like a person, to emergent conditions of history. Yet viewed from the vantage point of final judgment and justifying grace it is one body in Christ, a single apostolate, made holy by God's own sanctifying action. Confessional practice remains the same in the apostolic tradition, though its cultural form and language may alter in time.

Forms of administry in church history vary on a wide scale from relatively hierarchical to egalitarian patterns. Providence has worked by means of both monarchic and democratic governance, both spontaneous and designed, both charismatic and structured patterns of leadership, but never for long by either anarchy or tyranny. For anarchy is the absence of governance and tyranny is the undue excess of governance. Anarchy disdains power and tyranny seizes it. Anarchy has a deficiency of order and tyranny has an oversupply of it. Various historical ways of ordering have proven themselves relatively more fair and equitable than others, but none is absolutely just within the history of sin. The branches of the vine that lapse temporarily either into tyranny or anarchy in due time become broken and are cast off (Luther, LW 54:289ff., 3–8ff.; Reinhold Niebuhr, NDM I).

Administry may be relatively more hierarchical in one period and more populist in another, more elitist or democratic, more sacerdotal or lay oriented in one than another culture. But there is a variable deeper than any of these differences: It is the extent to which the body is enlivened through the Spirit and directed through its Head, the Son, to celebrate and refract the atoning love of the Father. What does not change in time is the organic relation of the body and the head, the relation of Christ to the church. The nature of the organism endures through variable adjustments to actual historical conditions.

The church's mission has come to us in unbroken descent from Christ and the apostles, but only by means of having negotiated countless historical circumstances with variable levels of faithful imagination, resourceful reasoning, and moral courage (Luther, LW 4:26ff.). Her survival, however, is not due to the fact that she was more clever than her detractors or more intrepid or ingenious, but that she is made alive by the Spirit to embody the continuing life of the crucified Lord of glory.

In relation to Christ, church governance resembles a benevolent sovereign. In relation to human community-building in proximate refraction of the holiness of God, the church at best resembles a self-constrained, constantly reordering, mutually-corrective, fair democratic process (Cambridge Platform, X, 1648, CC, p. 393).

# Complementary Models of Disciplinary Administry

Embryonic forms of various types of church government appear in Scripture: the "seven wise head" model of the Hebrew village system (Acts 6:3), the synagogue instructional system (Acts 13:14; 18:1–17); the overseer-director model (*episkopos*) of a beneficent leader (1 Tim. 3:2); the patronate model (*pater*) of the Romans; the president or elder (*presbyteros*) as a preeminent leader such as James of Jerusalem; and the superintendency (*hegoumenoi*) of missionaries, as with Titus in Crete. All these appear to be adapted at various times to the emergent mission of the church (Hooker, LEP III.3ff; Strong, ST, p. 897).

Christ commissioned and established the church and ordered it to mission, and the Spirit breathed life into it, authorizing the apostles to devise (and where necessary improvise) procedures, structures, and regulations fitting to changing times and unfolding multi-cultural circumstances. Considerable latitude was given to reason and moral prudence in relating the Gospel to changing societies, mutating languages, and exilic conditions. No single definitive form or theory of ecclesiastical management, supervision, governance, or discipline was fixed and defined for all cultures by apostolic teaching.

Adaptive arrangements that were intended to meet the special needs of the primitive Christian mission in its emergent cultural setting need not be regarded as absolutely normative for the church on all occasions and times in which radically different challenges emerge. Any procedure of governance consonant with apostolic teaching is permitted. It does not follow that because one theory or opinion of church governance is agreeable to Scripture, another is therefore false. "The Church of God of every place and every time has, according to its circumstances, the authority, power, and right to change, to diminish and to increase, without thoughtlessness and offence, in an orderly and becoming way, as at any time may be regarded best for good order" (Formula of Concord, 645, SCF, p. 406).

Christ offered himself to the church as its stabilizing center, leaving the apostolate free to choose varied means, procedures, and agencies to preach the good news, gather believers into community, order worship, edify moral experience, admonish and instruct according to Scriptures. Only two very simple rites—a bath and a meal—were enjoined by Christ to be the chief means of enabling grace for the church's mission. The presumption was on the side of freedom of conscience and contextual responsibility in determining the choice of other specific means to achieve the purposes of the church.

Circumcision was a formative example of an ecclesial decision in which a particular culture-specific practice was not forced upon all. Judaizing proponents sought to perpetuate circumcision among hellenistic Christian converts, as if necessary to salvation. At the point at which circumcision was asserted as a necessary work, Paul responded: "If you let yourselves be circumcised, Christ will be of no value to you at all" (Gal. 5:2; Luther, LW 27:329ff; cf. 26:411ff.). The new wine was destined to burst the old skins.

If a social organization is to be intentional, it must define what membership means, what rules regulate the society, and how its mission is to be ordered. The sacrament of new birth points to spiritual new birth, even if anticipatively. The formal profession that one is buried with Christ and risen with him in baptism marks the spiritual entrance of the person into the community of faith and participation in Christ's death and resurrection.

Donatist-tilting church governance wrongly imagined that one area (as in this case North Africa) could be arbitrarily detached from the ecumenical whole. By experience it became clear to the disciplined community that the unity and catholicity of the church required a baptismal discipline that prevailed ecumenically.

Nor could orthodox spirituality move in the antinomian direction of implying that it could accomplish its mission without instructing its members morally, or without corrective admonition of growing members. While the church has no coercive power to exercise as does the state, it does not simply tolerate any and all behaviors on the part of its members (M. Creighton, Persecution and Tolerance, pp. 126ff.).

# The Role of Disciplinary Decision Making and Consultative Proto-democracy in the Apostolic Tradition

When the apostolate found it necessary to appoint new officers, they "gathered all the disciples together" to make a decision (Acts 6:2). When the proposal was made for seven "full of the [Holy] Spirit" to be chosen for table service, "This proposal pleased the group" and they ("the multitude," KJV) proceeded to make the choices (Acts 6:5). One gets the impression that there was a relatively democratic spirit of cooperative, corporate consultation and decision-making in the Jerusalem church that was embodying the body of Christ.

That representatives may be delegated to assemblies to make conciliar decisions seems clear from the example of the church of Antioch, who did not go *en masse* to Jerusalem, but designated authorized representatives: "So Paul and Barnabas were appointed, along with some other believers, to go up to Jerusalem to see the apostles and elders" (Acts 15:2). Note that it was "the apostles and elders, *with the whole church"* who acted conjointly, sending Paul and Barnabas and others to the Gentile believers (Acts 15:22, italics added). This sort of affinity between apostolic tradition and general, populist, lay democratic expression of consent to the apostolic tradition has characterized classic Christian views of governance from the outset. Lay consent appears to be taken for granted when early bishops were appointed "with the approval of the whole church" (Clement of Rome, Corinth, 44, ECF, p. 33).

The second council of Constantinople gave explicit ecumenical definition to this long-standing tradition of popular consent derived from the apostles: "For although the grace of the Holy Spirit abounded in each one of the Apostles, so that no one of them needed the counsel of another in the execution of his work, yet they were not willing to define on the question then raised touching the circumcision of the Gentiles, until being gathered together they had confirmed their own several sayings by the testimony of the divine Scriptures. And thus they *arrived unanimously* at this sentence, which they wrote to the Gentiles: 'It has seemed good to the Holy Ghost and to us, to lay upon you no other burden than these necessary things'" (NPNF 2 XIV, p. 306, italics added, cf. Acts 15:28).

Christian offices of ministry arose largely as an extension and adaptation of the pattern of the synagogue elders, who studied and expounded Scripture, led in prayer, admonished the unruly, and administered discipline for the health of the community. These local organizations were to some degree self-governing. "No ruler is appointed over a congregation, unless the congregation is consulted" (Talmud, Berachob, 55a, Strong, ST, p. 902). If the authorization to administer discipline is grounded in general consent, the representative minister of the Word must not pretend to take the place of the church, or usurp legitimate authority of the people of God (Cyprian, Letters, FC 51, pp. 42–53, 97ff.).

Duly representative order is regularly preferred to absolute egalitarian fantasies: "That creation cannot be governed, or live, in a state of absolute equality, we are taught by the examples of the heavenly hosts, since, there being angels and also archangels, it is manifest that they are not equal, but in power and rank, as you know, one differs from another. If then among these who are without sin there is evidently this distinction, who of men can refuse to submit himself willingly to this order of things which he knows that even angels obey?" (Gregory the Great, Letters, LIV, NPNF 2 XII, p. 183).

In the body of Christ, each member is of great importance (Eph. 3, 4). No branch of the vine, no member of the body, can claim inherent superiority over the other. Both freedom and structure, both trusteeship and order, are presupposed in equitable measure in the maxim that one should be "eager to serve; not lording it over those entrusted to you" (1 Pet. 5:3). The call to servanthood echoes through Jesus' instructions: "But you are not to be called 'Rabbi,' for you have only one Master and you are all brothers" (Matt. 23:8). The seeds of classic procedures guaranteeing due process, equity, fairness, liberty, and proto-democracy were embryonically written into these texts, later to be more fully developed in the notion of liberty of conscience in matters of faith and morals. Constantine viewed his membership in the church as a higher authority than his leadership of the Roman empire.

In an effective democratic ethos the majority do well to govern with prudence, and humility, and the minority do well to dissent with constrained patience. In matters where policy decisions were not already clearly determined by scriptural mandates, a dialogical process is needed in which the consent of the whole community is referenced and sought (Acts 15:1–31). In discovering God's call through the hearing of the Word and prayer, each member enjoys the privilege of conscience-illumined judgment to a high degree, so long as that judgment is accountable to the body's head for its use of the means of grace (Gregory of Nyssa, Ag. Eunomius, I.36, NPNF 2 V, p. 85; Strong, ST, p. 900). The Roman clergy wrote to Cyprian their approval of "an assembly for counsel" which would include both clergy and laity (Cyprian, Letters, XXX, ANF V, p. 310). It was by a reassertion of the Cyprianic principle that constitutional process was sustained in the Council of Frankfort, 794, and in the medieval English tradition, and again recovered in Protestant polity (Cyprian, Epistles, LXXXII, ANF V, p. 409–412).

The principle of representative democratic guidance according to apostolic teaching was already firmly grasped by the Canons of Chalcedon: "If however by the common vote of all, founded upon reason, and according to the canons, two or three moved by their own obstinacy, make opposition, let the vote of the majority stand" (Session XVI, NPNF 2 XIV, p. 294).

However valuable an achievement constitutional democracy has been, it remains an exaggeration to imply that God works by this political means only. The nativistic voice of the people can be just as wrongly misdirected (as we see in the Third Reich and Islamic nationalist revolutions) as can monarchy or oligarchy.

# The Cross-cultural Variability of Confessional Practice

Strict uniformity in confessional practice "is neither possible, nor useful, nor necessary" (Hutter, Loci, 518). "Nor is it necessary that human traditions, rites or ceremonies, instituted by men, should be everywhere alike" (Augsburg Conf., VII, CC, p. 70). Some human traditions are valuable and not to be mocked or depreciated by the worshiping community. They bond the community, sanctify time, guide conscience, and deserve to be followed as *jure humano* even if not *jure divino*. "In the assembly readers could not all speak at once, but one after another, in order" (Augsburg Conf., XXVIII, CC, p. 103). The forgiving community is a setting in which it is hoped that all things, including the delicate duty of gentle admonition, can be done decently and in order.

Zwingli deliberately sought to do away with church fes-

festivals (excepting the Sabbath), opposing crosses, paintings, altars, bells, and decorations. This tradition was carried on further by some forms of Puritan and Reformed ecclesiology. Luther's tradition stressed that where God has made no command there must be liberty. Accordingly Lutheran and Anglican irenics have pleaded with Reformed and Puritan and pietistic advocates not to go too far in trying absolutely to clean up the church from all evidences of human design and human tradition and human forms of order and governance, for different cultures have different contributions and needs and gifts. Yet those rites and usages which cannot be observed without sin are to be avoided (Augsburg Apol., BOC, pp. 170–04; Formula of Concord, BOC, pp. 493–99). As there is no scripturally mandated obligation to celebrate Easter on a particular day, so there is not one prescribed rite of confession for all cultures, yet for the sake of good order we do well to yield to tested patterns rather than merely to assert individual liberty (Augsburg Apol., XXVI, in Neve, Luth. Sym., p. 243).

Ceremonies need not be unnecessarily multiplied. This applies to the repentance that is encouraged and enabled in the forgiving community. Rites of penitence are to be respected, especially where they have long standing and are not in conflict with Scripture, for "without a reasonable cause nothing in customary rites" need be changed (Formula of Concord, Apology, p. 227, 51; Neve, Luth. Sym., p. 243).

Rites and ceremonies are provided for the feeding of the flock by means of the testimony of Scripture, moral instruction, songs of praise, and the life of prayer. There is no intrinsic merit in mouthing words of confession simply as an end in itself. A ceremony, such as a rite of penance, does not profit simply because performed—*ex opere operato* (Augsburg Apol., BOC, pp. 173–76). A solemn warning accompanies all liturgical proceedings: Do not turn the gift of God's good news into the despair of a new legalism.

# Interlude: A Case of Conflicting Charges

I will attempt another case study for reflection, offered with the intent of drawing the issues of this chapter closer to the arena of confessional practice.

Pastor Carl Manning, a distinguished clergyman has been charged with sexual harassment by a group of abortionist-feminist activists. The charge is solicitation of sexual favors. There are indications that he is being set up, as punishment for his public opposition to abortion practices favored by the activists. You are on an investigation committee. The pastor has unequivocally denied all charges. His good character is widely attested by competent and trustworthy male and female associates.

The chairperson of the committee of inquiry is prone to discount evidence in his favor. You are in a minority in the committee. The momentum of the investigation is tilting toward a severe reprimand of a pastor who may be innocent, possibly a civil lawsuit for damages, and loss of ministerial credentials. A word is whispered that if you frustrate this momentum, you yourself might be similarly charged.

One of these activist is a members of your church. She comes to receive holy communion under your ministry. What is the relation between her moral actions and your responsibilities in rightly offering her holy communion? Is any form of discipline plausible? If so, how would such an admonition proceed, and on whose initiative?

You pray for discernment that you may ascertain a fitting pastoral response to this situation. What form of discernment to you would be most crucial?

# Recapitulation

Liturgical traditions understandably grew up expressing many varieties of cultural-historical differences within the one, holy, catholic, apostolic church.

It is the Holy Spirit who forms, orders, and configures the

community of worship, its preaching, prayer, sacramental life, and mission. This configuring functions practically by means of the work of administry—that form of ministry required to enable other forms of ministry. The Administrator of the diffusion of gifts is God the Holy Spirit.

From this premise grows the vine of disciplinary governance through historical change by responding to emergent historical conditions and demands. There is no single form of governance that applies to all historical situations, but rather an ever-emergent requirement to look for proximately just and useful forms of oversight in the light of specific historic limitations.

Whoever voluntarily accepts membership in the body of Christ thereby decides to be subject to its structures of discipline, admonition, and governance. Since the community is entered voluntarily, all its structures of discipline are wholly voluntary. The apostolic tradition from the outset has been earnest in its effort to welcome and enable informed consent to the word of forgiveness proclaimed. At its truer moments the reconciling community has been flexible in seeking consultative and proto-democratic modes of decision making consonant with the apostolic witness.

# 7

# Lay and Clergy Discipline
# Why the Distinction Persists

A series of questions on the relation of the community and its leadership emerged early in the apostolic tradition, and remain a challenge in subsequent centuries: It is puzzling as to how lay and clerical responsibilities interface in the administration of discipline. The *laos* is a single whole people to whom the *klēros* belongs, and to whom the *klēros* are assigned distinctive guardianship tasks.

Does the default of corrective discipline by a hypertolerationist clergy exempt the laity from accountability? At what point must the whole *laos* take initiative in setting aright the negligence of clergy in matters of discipline? How does the ministry of corrective love take place through the lay apostolate working through many vocations by which the leaven of forgiveness penetrates the world? How is the spiritual priesthood of the whole church enmeshed in the outworking of corrective love? What special obligations of admonition fall to the ordained clergy?

## Spiritual Priesthood of the Whole Church and the Ordered Ministry

"Spiritual priesthood" refers to the personal relation of immediate access to God the Father through Christ which is the privilege of every believer (1 Pet. 2:5–9; Origen, Hom. on Leviticus, IV.6; VI.5; IX. 1,8; XIII.5; Augsburg Apol., BC, pp. 214–24). This general spiritual lay priesthood is distinguished from ordained ministry in which the public proclamation of the Word and administration of the Sacrament is performed representatively for the whole church. The whole people of God is a spiritual priesthood (Calvin, Inst. 2.15).

Where two or three are called by the Gospel and gather faithfully in Christ's name (Matt. 18:20), there is the living body of Christ, the *ekklēsia*. This gathering does not emerge without apostolic testimony, hence without an ordered ministry of Word and Sacrament standing in continuity with the historic apostolate. There can be no ordained ministry without the people of God, and there is ordinarily no people of God without ordered ministry (Chemnitz, MWS, pp. 21–33). God "reconciled us to himself through Christ and gave us the ministry of reconciliation" (2 Cor. 5:18). The "us" referred to is clearly the whole body of the faithful who share in this ministry. Yet Paul also valued highly the office of apostle (Rom. 1:1–5), and of prophets, teachers, and evangelists (Eph. 4:11).

The body is one, yet not all members have the same function or range of accountability. All members are regarded as a "royal priesthood, a holy nation, a people belonging to God," hence summoned to "declare the praises of him who called you out of darkness into his wonderful light. Once you were not a people, but now you are the people of God" (1 Pet. 2:9; Chemnitz, MWS, p. 209). Becoming the people of God requires taking on the tasks of discipline that belong to that people.

The call to enter the body of Christ, and hence to the general ministry of the church, is visibly evidenced by repentance, faith, and baptism. The call to ordained ministry, which presupposes repentance, faith, and baptism but is not identical with them, is a call to representative ministry of Word, Sacrament, and pastoral admonition (Luther, Babylonian Captivity, WML II, p. 283). The minister acts for the church and within the apostolic tradition in exercising the commissioned authority to open the door of God's forgiveness to the penitent and close it to the impenitent.

Ordained ministry comes into being by virtue of God's call, not in the first instance by the local congregation's or preacher's call. "The exercise of ecclesiastical power, in calling and electing ministers, in loosing and binding sins, is in the name and by the authority of the entire Church" (Gerhard, LT VI, 57, SCD, p. 429; cf. Council of Neocaesarea, NPNF 2 XIV, pp. 79–84; John Chrysostom, On the Priesthood).

# Laos and Klēros as One People Being Made Holy

All the baptized are formed into one people (*laos*) who are in the process of renewal, becoming the body of Christ, the temple of the Spirit. The laity are not merely those who are not clergy, but the whole people of God. The functional distinction between *laos* and *klēros* is not meant to divide but unite the single body in orderly mission (Cyprian, Letters, FC 51, pp. 42ff., 110ff.). *Klēros* serves within the whole people of God, not above or over against them.

Christ himself has called into being and ordered a missional, visible *koinonia* that includes lay persons in general ministry, and a representative ministry to serve this general ministry through Word and Sacrament and pastoral care. Such an order is needed to insure that the laity are not deprived of the means of grace necessary and sufficient for salvation, which is their right as people adopted into the family of God.

There is no *ekklēsia* without *klēsis*, no assembly without being called by God into being and order, no ordered church without called leadership. Distinguishable tasks are entrusted to the *klēros*, but only in order to ensure and enable the health of the whole *laos* (Luther, Babylonian Captivity, WML II, pp. 282ff.).

The distinction between *laos* (the whole people) and *klēros* (those duly chosen and assigned to serve and represent the whole) has proven perennially useful to the order of the church and a consequence of our obedience to Christ. Those serving in ordering ministries are chosen, not self-choosing. For the root word of *klēros* carries the nuance of "a lot" (Heb:

*goral*), or that which is chosen as if by lot—by divine calling—from the *laos* (Neh. 10:34; Jonah 1:7). The lot was employed as an act of meekness and piety in order to reduce contentiousness (Prov. 18:18). In the choosing the successor to Judas, "the lot (*klēros*) fell to Matthias; so he was added to the eleven apostles" (Acts 1:26; Calvin, Comm. XVIII, pp. 70-72).

The *laos* have all the same range of saving graces pertaining to salvation that the *klēros* have. The benefits of repentance, faith, and baptism are equally shared by all. The *laos/klēros* distinction is not a spiritual or religious difference, but a functional differentiation of order wherein some, being allotted a particular duty and guardianship, are by due process set aside and called for representative ministries on behalf of the whole people (Luther, Commentary on Psalm 110, LW 13, p. 332).

The task of *klēros* is to build up the body of Christ, so that in their vocations the laity can penetrate the world with the forgiving Word. The *laos* in being edified is charged with the proximate forming of the environing culture within the conditions of the history of sin (Peter Chrysologus, Sermons, 108, FC 17, pp. 168–9).

Gross misconceptions have followed in the trail of a misunderstanding of this premise. For clergy have mistakenly thought it their duty to enter the political arena and engage in shameless direct lobbying, influence-peddling, media-sensitive demonstration politics, partisan money-raising activities, and even divisive insurgency movements, rather than to take on the more demanding and necessary task of the sacred ministry of Word and Sacrament. By this the reputation of the *klēros* has been smudged, and some time and penitence will be needed for its recovery.

If some are made teachers or shepherds on behalf of the welfare of others, the purpose is that all may share more effectively in the common body of the faithful and become more completely the temple of the Spirit (Cyprian, Unity of the Church, FC 36, pp. 95-121; Hugh of St. Victor, On Sacr., II.2, pp. 253-59). Whatever distinction may be usefully made between *laos* and *klēros* to secure the ministry of the whole, each one shares equally in a unifying purpose to bring health to the whole body in service to the world (Doc. Vat. II, Ch 32, pp. 58–59).

Already within the first century, Clement of Rome was distinguishing between "precepts pertaining to the laity" and "duties incumbent upon the Levites" or priestly order. "Let each of us, brethren, 'in his own order' with a good conscience not transgressing the prescribed rule of his own office give thanks to God honorably" (Clement, Corinth, 41, SCD 42, p. 20; cf. 1 Cor. 15:23).

# How Corrective Love Functions within the Representative Ministry

Christ chose the Twelve from the disciples, and they in turn appointed and ordained elders, overseers, and deacons to enable and actualize the mission of the church. These he instructed and empowered by the Holy Spirit to proclaim, teach, intercede representatively, and guide. The recipients of the tradition communicated this mission to later generations of leaders who were similarly authorized to proclaim, intercede, and guide the church (Clement of Rome, Corinth, 40-59, ANF I, pp. 16–20).

In this way the mission of the church from the outset has been implemented transgenerationally by a functional distinction between the lay apostolate and an ordained apostolate duly consecrated by the laying on of hands. This ordering of the church into the ministry of the laity and the representative ministry of those ordained to sacred ministry is arguably either intrinsic to the nature of the church, or at very least it has been assumed by the Christian community from its earliest times. There remains no substantial memory of a called out people without some ordered leadership of the holy community. Though particular offices are arguably not necessary to the very *being* of the church, "yet ordinarily to their calling they are" necessary to the church's *well-being* (Cambridge Platform, CC, p. 392).

In the earliest descriptions of the *ekklēsia* there is a functional distinction between the people (*laos*) and their duly called and designated elders, representatives, guides, or pastors (Clement, Romans 1; Ignatius, Trallians 3; Didache, 15; Cyprian, Epistle 66; Augustine, CG XX.10). Viewed as a body politic (*congregatio politica*), the ordered church consists of laity and clergy, the whole body and the ordained ministry.

The notion of "hierarchy" comes from the Greek *hierarchēs*, a steward or keeper of sacred things who guides a religious community (Journet, CWI, pp. 16–50). Until the rise of representative democracy in the 18th century, the prevailing rule was that "the best government of a multitude is that it be ruled by one" (Tho. Aq., SCG, IV.76, p. 291). Even amid an egalitarian ethos it remains true that the best achievements of democracy cannot occur without some sort of hierarchical order, classification of station, and distinctions of chain of command, rank, seniority, standing, and accountability.

It is to an ordered ministry that the task of guiding the whole body falls, so that the apostolate is brought in touch with particular historical conditions. As physicians of souls they apply the medicine of the Sacraments (Ambrose, The Mysteries, 8, FC 44, pp. 20-28; Bonaventure, Breviloqium, 6.12).

# Limits of Pastoral Discipline

"What I am for you terrifies me," Augustine confessed to his congregation concerning the responsibilities of his office, but "what I am with you consoles me. *For you* I am a bishop; but *with you* I am a Christian. The former is a title of *duty*; the latter, one of *grace*. The former is a *danger*; the latter, *salvation*" (Sermons, 340.1, MPL 38, p. 1483, italics added; Doc. Vat. II, Ch 32, p. 59).

The ordinal prerogative is best upheld by the pastor "who

knows how both to maintain it and to combat it," wrote Gregory. If it should happen that the pastor views lay persons "whom he has surpassed in the accident of power" as if he had transcended them "also in the merits of his life," a great disaster ensues (Gregory the Great, BPR, NPNF 2 XII, p. 14).

Some in sacred ministry may for a time become bewitched by the antinomian fantasy that they as clergy are in some measure exempt from elementary lay disciplines (like paying bills, telling the truth, showing up on time, being faithful to one's spouse, etc.). Ordination sometimes escalates these temptations. Far from being exempt from the same discipline expected of the *laos*, as representative officers and public spokespersons for the laity, they have those same levels of accountability plus additional responsibilities not shared by laity.

Hence there is a special sphere of discipline required of representative ministers of Word and Sacrament. This is why a conceptual distinction is useful between the discipline of church members and the discipline of persons in the ordered ministry. Double standard? No, for it assumes that the behavioral standard expected of the laity will at least be followed by the clergy, and in addition those responsibilities voluntarily assumed in ordination.

The disciplining of pastors and church officers focuses primarily upon the continuance or non-continuance of their authorization to act in representative ministry for the whole church—whether they can be entrusted with the ministry of Word and Sacrament and care of souls. A long tradition of due process has followed the interpretation of the text: "Do not entertain an accusation against an elder unless it is brought by two or three witnesses" (1 Tim. 5:19). If the church loses the capacity or courage to surveil and call to accountability unfaithful ministers, vast consequences follow for the neglected laity.

# The Strategic Positional Advantage of Lay Ministries in the World

The laity are not charged or encumbered with the special requirements of the pastoral office of ordained ministry, for which clergy must give radical account to God at final judgment (Ezek. 34). Laity are thereby free to do what they are strategically positioned best to do: to serve in the middle of worldly structures to embody and attest God's love for the world. On no single person's shoulders does the entire mission of the church toward the world fall (1 Cor. 12). That should be a comfort to those who take their vocation too seriously. Yet in each moment, each believer is called to penetrate the bleak world of sin with the light of God's own sanctity and holiness, righteousness and justice (John 1:1–9). While the reform of ministry is primarily the responsibility of ministers, it is of deep interest and importance to the laity, and at times becomes a matter of direct lay concern and action.

The regular setting in which the laity participate in Christ's priestly ministry is in the responsive hearing of the word in common worship and in sharing in the Eucharist. The Supper with the Lord is rightly celebrated by all laity who, having been called, make their whole life an offering to God for others (Acts 2:42–47; Rom. 12:1; 1 Pet. 3:15; cf. Schmaus, *Dogma* 4, p. 123).

The laity have full rights to receive the means of grace instituted by Christ from the spiritual shepherds appointed by due process to proclaim the Word and administer the Sacraments. At any time any lay persons may feel themselves called upon to express their distinctive experience-based insights for the good of the whole body. This expression usually proceeds through ordinary means and structures of governance and community, and by special petition when necessary.

Prudently and charitably the laity are called to offer the church their best wisdom, prudential judgment, and resources, whatever they may be. In return they owe accountability and disclosure to their spiritual shepherds. They are called to pray for those who watch over them, who themselves are in turn called to give account to God for their watchfulness (Ezek. 34; cf. Heb. 13:17; Wesley, WJW VII, pp. 108-17; Vat. II, Ch 37).

As nerves reach to all parts of the body from the head enabling them power to feel and move, so the Head of the Church communicates power to the body by enlightening the mind and conferring grace (Pius XII, Mystici Corporis, 49–51, pp. 30–32).

# Daily Testimony of the Lay Apostolate through Vocations in the World

The lay apostolate participates in the care of souls by prayer, by the search for political justice, and by leading lives that show forth Christ's living presence in the world (Doc. Vat. II, Lai, pp. 489ff.; Balt. Catech., 151, p. 114). What specifically characterizes the laity is their propitious social location already in the middle of the life of the world (Doc. Vat. II, Ch 31, p. 57). Their light shines out most exquisitely when it beams precisely refracted through their concrete vocations within the world. Through each one all may see God's good works and glorify the Father in heaven (Matt. 5:16). "Live such good lives among the pagans that, though they accuse you of doing wrong, they may see your good deeds and glorify God on the day he visits us" (1 Pet. 2:12).

The lay apostolate thrives amid the concreteness of lay vocations in the world (Vat. II, Lai 1). Only through this concretely intermixed and blended relatedness can the church become salt of the earth (Matt. 5:13; Vat. II, Ch 33). The laity make the church palpably present in the life of the world.

The people of God "must be to the world what the soul is to the body" (Epistle to Diognetus, 6; Chrysostom, Hom. on Matt. 46.2; MPG 58, p. 478)—giving life to the world. The laity are better positioned than the clergy to disperse and spread throughout the world the reconciling life which assuages the poor, encourages the meek, suffers for righteousness sake, and makes peace (Matt. 5:3–9; CMM, pp. 222, 223).

The laity share in Christ's prophetic and public ministry by the daily testimony of their lives, which manifests their baptism, and the efficacy of the eucharistic table. This testimony flows into and permeates the whole of their family life, but also their responsible participation in the economic order through commerce and services, their political lives, their friendships, and their sharing in the formation of the culture they are given (John Chrysostom, Hom. on Matt. 46.2, NPNF 1 X, pp. 289–90; MPG 58, p. 478; Congar, Lay People in the Church).

By this daily testimony one is given ample opportunity to witness to the justice, holiness, and the love of God (2 Cor. 3:2–3). The laity from the outset have offered this daily testimony through their deeds and words (Justin Martyr, Dialogue with Trypho, 3, ANF I, pp. 195–96; Second Letter of Clement).

Persuasive testimony to Christ is most convincingly made by those whose daily lives manifest honest correspondence between their words and their behavior (1 Cor. 13; Rom. 16:17–19). Although the public task of formally and authoritatively proclaiming God's word ordinarily belongs to the representative ministry, this office is shared with laity, especially where teaching charisms are evident.

In his 18th year, when he was still a layman, before Origen was ordained presbyter, he "took charge of the catechetical school" and became a renowned interpreter of Scripture (Eusebius, CH, 6.3–8, NPNF 2 I, pp. 251–55). In periods where lay testimony has fallen into relative quiescence, it has been again and again mightily revived (Clare of Assisi, CWS, pp. 226–32; Early Dominicans, CWS; Wesley, WJWB, Sermons, vol. 2, pp. 73–76; Phoebe Palmer, "Laity for the Times," New York Christian Advocate and Journal, 1857). In the traditions of both east and west, lay teachers have steadily remained integral to the church's teaching mission.

# Whether Women Are Called to Admonition and Counsel

The New Testament did not limit women to duties of family and household. In early Christianity women often prophesied (Cf. Acts 2:17–18; 21:9; Rom. 16:1–2; Num. 11:29; 2 Kings 22:14; 1 Cor. 12:28; Eph. 4:11). In some instances Paul prohibited women from public teaching (1 Cor. 14:34–35). He prohibited women from prophesying unveiled and from usurping legitimate authority (1 Cor. 11:5–13). The passage often thought to be most definite in rejecting women's ordination is 1 Tim. 2:8–12. Paul clearly was commending the virtue of *hesuchia* (quietness) to women in worship, as he also was commending a tranquil spirit of prayer to men (See Oden, IBC: First and Second Timothy and Titus, pp. 91–102).

Paul's first public proclamation in Europe was to a group of gathered women "outside the city gate" by the river at Philippi. His first convert in Europe was a woman named Lydia (Acts 16:9–15). At the head of a long list of greetings in Romans 16, Paul commended to Rome "our sister Phoebe" who was "also a servant of the church in Cenchrea" (*kai diakonon tēs ekklēsias*), and a protectress (*prostatis*) of many (Rom. 16:1–2). Women were employed as teachers (Titus 2:3–4). Pliny spoke of deaconesses as exercising functions analogous to deacons.

Contrary to the Jewish practice of initiatory rites only for males in circumcision, women were not only baptized but baptized others (Council of Carthage, IV, XII, NPNF 2 XIV, p. 41). Women were the first to proclaim the good news of Jesus' resurrection to doubting male disciples (Matt. 28:7–9, 17). "She, while apostles shrank, could danger brave; Last at the cross, and earliest at his grave" (Binney, TCI, p. 195; cf. Matt. 26:56; Matt. 27:55,56; 28:1; Elizabeth Schüssler-Fiorenza, In Memory of Her).

It was his sister Macrina who took Basil "in hand, and with such speed did she draw him also toward the mark of philosophy that he forsook the glories of this world"

(Gregory of Nyssa, Life of St. Macrina, p. 27, CCC, p. 104). Jerome's most rigorous Scripture student at Rome was Marcella, of whose death he wrote in a poignant letter: "Whatever in me was the fruit of long study and as such made by constant meditation a part of my nature, this she tasted, this she learned, and made her own. Consequently after my departure from Rome, in case of a dispute arising as to the testimony of Scripture on any subject, recourse was had to her to settle it" (Jerome, Letters, 127.7, CCC, p. 186).

# The Voluntary Consent of the Laity to Apostolic Discipline

It is for the whole people of God that the Word of God is sent, offered up, and received. Only the whole people of God can offer the consensus that is required for ecumenical teaching (Vincent of Lerins, Commonitory, 1,2 NPNF 2 XI, pp. 128–32). Lacking reasonable ecumenical historic consent, any scriptural teaching remains subject to further inquiry, accompanied by intercession for illumination.

When the question of circumcision needed to be decided by the precedent-setting council of Jerusalem, "The apostles and elders met to consider this question" (Acts 15:6). This appears to have been a deliberative body inclusive of laity, yet a body in which some voices would on the basis of their memory, experience, and calling take special roles. It is clear from verse 12: "The *whole assembly* became silent as they listened to Barnabas and Paul." The people of the church were not excluded from this deliberation. Verse 22 then makes the point even clearer that a larger body than apostles and elders were present: "Then the apostles and elders, *with the whole church*, decided to choose some of their own men and send them to Antioch" (Acts 15:22, italics added). The "whole church" at Jerusalem meant the laity, who were involved in this decision-making proto-democratic process in the mode of consent to apostolic teaching, as Cyprian later recalled, "with the general advice" of the laity (Cyprian,

Epistles, XXXII, ANF V, p. 312; Dorner, SCDoc., IV, p. 333).

None of the Ecumenical Councils of the early church became so until the whole *laos* accepted their pronouncements. The Robber Council (Ephesus, 449), and the Iconoclasts' Council (754) were both called with the full intention of being "ecumenical," and with substantial episcopal representation, but the *laos* as a whole clearly rejected their decisions.

As with the natural body, no member has a free ride, lacking responsibilities within the body. At some point each cell, each muscle, each nerve, is called upon in its own due time to perform its function for the whole, and thus be formed in the likeness of the Head, "until Christ is formed in you" (Gal. 4:19). Each member is given life in the body to be made like the Head, die and be raised with him, and finally to share in his glory and governance (Eph. 2:6; Phil. 3:21; 2 Tim. 2:11). The gradual forming of the cell or member in correspondence with the Head begins with baptism (as a kind of birth) and continues to be nurtured through communion with the Head (Col. 2:12; Schmaus, Dogma 4, p. 115).

# Interlude: A Case of Habitual Lying

Marge has a mischievous habit of telling lies and breaking commitments. Her pastor has observed this pattern on several occasions. She has agreed to serve as a seventh-grade church school teacher. On her first Sunday of responsibility she called in sick, but promised that she would certainly be there the following Sunday. She did not appear. The next Monday a parishioner inadvertently mentioned to the pastor that she had seen Marge at Flea Market both Sundays. The next morning there is a knock on the door. Marge is standing in the doorway. Should she be confronted?

# Recapitulation

In the administration of discipline, lay and clerical responsibilities always interface and interdepend. The *laos* is a single whole people to whom the *klēros* are assigned distinctive guardianship tasks. The default of corrective discipline by the ordained clergy does not finally exempt the laity from accountability, since the whole *laos* remains responsible for attending to its own health.

It is only through the lay apostolate working through many vocations that the leaven of the Gospel penetrates the world. No doctrine is made orthodox simply by clerical definition, but only by consent to apostolic testimony.

# Prospectus

We have advanced to the more demanding steps of this journey. Much of what we have covered thus far is preliminary spade work for the rigorous theological seed-planting that still lies ahead: Lay persons must understand anew why the decontamination of a corrupted clergy is their concern and burden. For this a proper groundwork must be laid.

Many mainline theological education institutions, now troubled by identity confusions, will not be modified without considerable lay empathy, commitment, and informed courage. The laity often stand in a better position than clergy to see undefensively what fair governance requires. If laity lack a grasp of this biblical-historical-theological groundwork, it may remain unclear how much the laity have at stake in the recovery of church discipline, fair governance, and the reordering of sacred ministry.

The entire curriculum of theological education would be significantly affected by a serious reexamination of confession: In biblical studies, the Scriptures would again be searched to understand the dynamics of guilt, sin, and forgiveness. The historical tradition of penitential practice has been poorly and prejudicially understood by Protestants. This inquiry would reshape church history courses. The doctrines of the intergenerational transmission of sin, the efficacy of atonement, and classic doctrines of sacrifice and forgiveness have received all too little attention in the chic liberated seminary. These questions need to be reinvestigated in theological curricula. Homiletics classically reconceived will help young pastors gain the courage to confront sin, admonish waywardness, challenge malevolence, and make witness over against prevailing cultural idolatries. The recovery of liturgical forms of confession, absolution, and the nurture of the Christian life await more careful study in seminaries. The answer lies not merely sending people to a six week clinical pastoral education exercise which psychologizes sin and reduces all spiritual problems to psychotherapeutic treatments. CPE itself must now come to terms with the classic Christian understanding of penance, repentance, confession, and divine forgiveness.

# 8

# Retrieving the Apostolic Practice of Admonition

How is the apostolic ministry to be nurtured through the unendingly varied seasons of cultural transformation? How, without diminishing its dynamic, is the apostolic testimony to be shepherded through the hazards of rapid social change? Will an ordered ministry forever remain an expression of the Spirit's work of corrective love? How is the unique hermeneutic of orthodoxy to be guarded and extended without dilution? Do all who voluntarily share in the body of Christ by their intentional confirmation of their baptism place themselves under the discipline of an ordered ministry? How did the personal relation between Jesus and his disciples decisively shape the offices of ministry? These are questions we now address.

## Why an Ordered Ministry Is Serviceable to the Spirit's Work of Corrective Love

In order to answer these questions it is necessary to reflect more intentionally upon the essential character of the apostolate, the seasonability of admonition, the meaning of sacred orders, the application of ecclesial discipline, the theological ground rules for the proximate reform of ecclesia, the optimal configuration of church governance, the leavening of the political order, and finally the pivotal importance of thoroughgoing reform of ministry and theological education. That is the energetic calisthenic that lies ahead.

The fidgety reader may be muttering: So how does this pertain to me? Why must I plow through all this arcane talk about apostolicity and discipline? Answer: The reform of the *ekklēsia* is finally the bedrock responsibility of the laity, especially when liberal clergy have been chronically derelict in guardianship duties. So we must repair to an elementary lay literacy course in the mission of apostolate.

## The Great Commission to the Apostolate

The defining text is precise:

All authority in heaven and on earth has been given to me. Therefore go and make disciples of all nations, baptizing them in the name of the Father and of the Son and of the Holy Spirit, and teaching them to obey everything I have commanded you. And surely I am with you always, to the very end of the age (Matt. 28:18–20).

This authorization embraces the whole range of apostolic activity. The ensuing mission is addressed to all people groups, all languages, every conceivable culture— commanding the gathered community to teach and baptize in the triune name from here to eternity, and promising the continuing presence of the living Lord (cf. Mark 13:10; 16:15; Schmaus, Dogma 4, pp. 30-32). "If you love me, you will obey what I command" (John 14:15).

Making disciples is integral to the very nature of the church. There can be no authentic preaching without the effort to make disciples. Baptizing implies discipling. Mission requires discipling. Where admonition languishes, mission flounders.

Long-standing barriers had to be penetrated to follow this command. The first was right next door in Samaria.

## The Initial Passage: To Samaria

The risen Lord commanded his disciples: "You will be my witnesses in Jerusalem, and in all Judea and Samaria, and to the ends of the earth" (Acts 1:8). The first transition from Jerusalem to Samaria would be no small hurdle.

Conflict between Jews and Samaritans dated to the Babylonian captivity, when some of those Jews left behind intermarried with colonists. John's Gospel observed the blunt sociological fact that "Jews do not associate with Samaritans" (John 4:9). It was this barrier, recalling a long memory of alienation, that Jesus directly broke through. When he told the great parable of binding up of the wounds of a stranger, the rescuer was a Samaritan (Luke 10:29–37). The Samaritans were those thought least ready to hear God's good news of salvation. The intent was insult when Jesus was called "a Samaritan and demon-possessed" (John 8:48). The task of evangelization would tackle just such barriers. The Spirit would penetrate such obstinacy. But how far? To the ends of the earth.

## The Time of the Apostolate

The time of the apostolate begins with the ascension and ends only with the general resurrection. The commission is to make disciples of all, baptizing and teaching "to the very end of the age" knowing that the Son is "with you always" by the power of the Spirit (Matt. 28:19,20), who will "guide you into all truth" (John 16:13) and empower the apostolic mission (Acts 1:8).

Apostolicity remains a defining mark of the gathered faithful of each generation. It is a pivotal evidence by which one tests whether the attestor bears true or false witness—by asking whether the testimony is in accord with apostolic testimony, whether one teaches what the apostles taught, whether this one is sent on the same mission as were the first apostles (Luther, LW 23:185ff.).

The test of apostolicity, however, turns out to be more than using the right words. For language can deceive as well as disclose. As Athanasius found out in the case of Arius, it is dangerous and tricky to assume that the apostolicity of a community can be tested merely by its language, for its language may sound apostolic without bearing the fruits of apostolicity (Athanasius, NPNF 2 I passim).

The church that forgets or falsifies Hebrew Scripture and the apostolic interpretation of it cannot be the apostolic church. Those who purport to be Christian teachers but bear testimony contrary to apostolic teaching fail to display a distinctive mark that defines the church. An alleged *ekklēsia* that lacks the mark of apostolicity might continue to live parasitically for a while off the vital residual wisdoms of the apostolic tradition while practically ignoring apostolic teaching, but that in time will spend itself, as we have seen repeatedly in history, as in its latest mutation in spent modernity.

It is God's own Spirit who actively undergirds and guards the accurate recollection of apostolic testimony. Subsequent generations of attestors are perennially pledged and bound to recall accurately and noninvasively the salvation event as received (Luther, LW 27:163ff.).

# The Mission of the Apostolate

None were chosen in the first generation of the disciplined apostolate without having accompanied Jesus personally during his earthly journey, without having met the risen Lord, and without being personally commissioned by him to testify reliably to his humanity, deity, and saving work. These elements were constitutive of the first generation of the apostolate, whose recollection subsequent generations of the apostolate are ever anew pledged to transmit (Luther, LW 36163ff., 41:311ff.).

The succeeding church is described by Paul as the pillar and ground of the truth (1 Tim. 3:15), God's own appointed means of upholding Christian testimony in the world. Christ entrusted the keys of discipline to the apostles and their successors, authorized the great commission, and sent the Spirit to empower their mission (Augustine, Concerning Faith of Things Not Seen, 10, NPNF 1 III: 341–43).

Apostolicity is intrinsically interwoven with the other marks of the church: Only that church which is one in the

Lord can be universal in mission. Only that church which is united in the one mission of the one Lord can be apostolic. Only that church which is formed by the apostolic memory can be united in one body with the Lord. Lacking that holiness which is fitting to the obedience of faith, one finds neither apostolicity nor universality of mission.

The church is apostolic insofar as it retains, guards, and faithfully transmits its apostolic mission. Those sent by the Son are the apostolate. As Christ was sent by the Father, the apostles were sent, empowered by the Spirit, and the continuing apostolate is still being sent. The apostolate is sent on the authority of the Son to whom "all authority in heaven and on earth has been given" (Matt. 28:18), to engage in the mission of the Son by the power of the Spirit. "As the Father has sent me, I am sending you" (John 20:21).

Jesus is the primary type of the apostle, as the one sent by the Father. "When the time had fully come, God sent his Son" (Gal. 4:4, Luther, LW 27:65ff.). "Therefore, holy brothers, who share in the heavenly calling, fix your thoughts on Jesus, the apostle" (Heb. 3:1; Luther, LW 29:143ff.). Jesus is the consummate apostle in the sense of being commissioned and authorized by God the Father and sent into the world.

The apostolate does not merely *have* a mission; it *is* a mission—the historical embodiment of the mission of God the Son through God the Spirit. As body of Christ the church embodies the mission of her Lord.

The church does not elect to engage in mission; rather the mission of God engages the church. The church does not elicit the mission, but rather the mission elicits and empowers the church. *Missio Dei* embraces all that the church is and does in its life in the world. This called-out community has a key role to play in the history of the emerging reign of God.

Some complain that if the church focuses attention on its own apostolicity it will tend to forget its mission to the world, as if caring for its own identity would stand as a threat to expressing its identity in mission. Any notion of apostolicity that fails to engage in mission is a misreading of apostolic memory of the Lord. The subtler danger is the failure to get one's own identity straight as one moves toward the ever-evolving mission in the world. To transform the world, the sent church must first understand what it means to be the church, else it simply becomes an anemic reflection of the idolatrous world (Augustine, On the Profit of Believing 18–23, NPNF 1 III:355–57).

# The Cross-Cultural Agility of Orthodoxy

The most salient feature of orthodoxy is not its rigidity but its flexibility centered in life in the Lord, its willingness to enter into this and that culture on behalf of its all-embracing mission. Apostolicity does not imply a rigid lack of adaptability to varied culture formations. The glory of the apostolic tradition is precisely its readiness to reach out, meet, confront, and dialogue with different cultures, to become all things to all on behalf of Christ (1 Cor. 9:19–22; Luther, LW 27:202).

Orthodoxy is not characterized by inflexibility or a woodenness incapable of varied responses. Rather it is freed to variable cultural responsiveness by being centered in the eternal Word. The living body of Christ lives by penetrating and transforming each new form of cultural life emergent in human history.

Because cultures and languages are constantly changing, and because the apostolic testimony must be attested in ever-new circumstances, it is a necessary feature of the apostolic tradition that it both guard the original testimony and make it understandable in new cultural settings. Failing either is to default on the apostolic tradition. Far from implying unbending immobility, apostolicity requires constant adaptation of the primitive apostolic testimony to new historical challenges and languages, yet without altering or diluting the primitive witness.

## Retrieving the Canon

Contemporary witnesses are called to assess every subsequent testimony by its correspondence with the original testimony of the apostles. The working premise is that the Holy Spirit would not allow a truly debilitating or defective testimony to be transmitted permanently to the church. Like music the words of the apostles are savored repeatedly by the remembering *ekklēsia*, wrote John Chrysostom.

It is not we who creatively decide what is apostolic but the apostles. The contemporary apostolate exists only because it has decided that the testimony of the apostles is true. If the record of their testimony is fundamentally flawed or defective, there is no way the church can begin to learn the truth, for the truth about God's own coming is attested only by original eyewitnesses as trustworthy attestors, and these are called the apostles (Luther, LW 11:259ff.).

Surely the Holy Spirit would not leave such an important matter up to the jaded imagination of tired tenured radicals speculating about form-criticism. The academic cartel of selected guild scholars who sat for decades on the Dead Sea Scrolls has only recently been broken up. Now it is time to say to the form-critical guild scholars who pretend to serve a guardianship function with the New Testament text: Give us back our canon.

Does modern historical criticism represent a devastating challenge to the principle of apostolicity? Briefly answered, no. When criticism is working well, so that an orthodox skepticism places in question the speculations of the historical critics, there is nothing to fear from solid historical inquiry into the tradition of transmission of apostolic testimony. There is only the task of improving historical inquiry and bringing it ever closer to the facts of the incarnate, risen Lord and his body, the church.

# The Founding of Ministry Ordered toward Evangelical Discipline: The Training of the Twelve

It is Christ who orders the church. His invitation to share in his body already contains within it the rudiments of visible community under a common rule, proficient leadership, temporal accountability, and orderly organization—all elements that are subject to historical development and cultural interface.

Already by the time of writing of the synoptic Gospels there was assumed a partially differentiated ministry, ordered by the Lord according to his purpose. Jesus chose the twelve to be witnesses to his life and teaching; he prepared and sent them to proclaim the good news of the kingdom (Mark 3:13–19; John 15:16; A. B. Bruce, The Training of the Twelve).

They were sent out in an intentional way, first to testify to the lost sheep of the house of Israel that "the kingdom of heaven is near" (Matt. 10:7), then to the Gentiles. The Twelve were not commissioned to improve upon Jesus' proclamation or invent an original or convenient adaptation, but to proclaim it as taught, remembering that " a student is not above his teacher" (Matt. 10:24). "After this the Lord appointed seventy-two others and sent them two by two ahead of him to every town and place where he was about to go," asking the Lord of harvest "to send out workers into his harvest field" (Luke 10:1–2; Luther, LW 23:186ff.).

The authority of the apostles functioned with general church consent. Their special place was regarded as derived from their unique companionship with Jesus, their reliable attestation of his life, death, and resurrection, and their being sent and commissioned by him. The modern fantasy that the apostles derived their authority on the basis of simple egalitarian assumptions or individualistic inspiration is hard to find in the New Testament text, and one must virtually eviscerate the text to wrench anything like this out of it.

We can say neither that the apostles existed before the church, nor the church before the apostles, for in the New Testament *apostolos* and *ekklēsia* emerged every step together, organically, in unison, the one guiding and the other consenting to apostolic guidance. Hence it is ill-advised to think chronologically of ministry as distinctly prior to the church, or the church as wholly prior to ministry (Ignatius, To the Smyrneans; Beveridge, Synodikon).

## Synagogue and *Ekklēsia* in Jerusalem as Primitive Models for Discipline and Governance

The basic model of ecclesial governance was the synagogue. The synagogue model had its greatest effect upon the church in its earliest decades and especially in its very first decade (A.D. 30–40). The governance of the Jewish synagogue sheds light on the formation of the early patterns of church leadership. As the church borrowed and transmuted from the synagogue its basic pattern of public worship, so did it borrow and attune and recast its offices, polity, and organization plan to the new circumstances of the world mission of the apostolate.

As remembered in Acts, it was a relatively short time after Pentecost that the church was furnished with a ministry similar in constitution and design to that which is found abundantly in prevailing patterns of ordered ministry today. The mother church in Jerusalem selected deacons and presbyters (Acts 6; 11:30; 15:2) by analogy with the synagogue (J.B. Lightfoot, CM, pp. 149–53; Chas. Gore, C&M, p. 239), with James as overseer (as implied in Acts 12:17; 15:13–19). The earliest Christian community in Jerusalem thus became the proximate norm for other communities of faith as they were forming (Luther, LW 40:389ff.; 41:72ff.).

In accord with this Jerusalem church pattern, the early Christian missionaries such as Paul found it reasonable to appoint presbyters and deacons in the churches they planted.

This took more time in some instances than in others, since the process had to be organically related to particular local developments and challenges.

In the synagogue the congregation dealt with offenses against the community, either by requiring almsgiving or through expulsion, or in some cases corporal punishment. Synagogue practice was modified by the Christian community, where forms of discipline varied from place to place, but frequently called for fasting or almsgiving or public confession of sin.

## The Eldership Model Appropriated by *Presbyteroi*

Each synagogue had a circle of rulers or elders (*presbyteroi*), of whom one was elected presiding elder, who superintended public worship, taught the Scriptures, offered prayers representatively for the whole congregation, and blessed the people. Elders were referred to as "rulers of the synagogue." They sat in a semicircle facing the people in the synagogue, so that visually there was in worship a clear ordering of the community into the larger body of the gathered people of God as resonant with their spiritual guides. "The elders sit with their faces toward the people, and their backs to the place where the law is deposited" wrote Maimonides (Watson, TI, p. 579). It is probable that early Christian believers also sat facing their leaders who read and expounded the Scripture.

Jewish elders were ordained by the laying on of hands and by prayer, as distinguished from Levitical priests, who were not ordained but rather came to their office by birth. Thus the primary model for Christian ministry was taken less directly from temple than synagogue. It was thought capable of being recalibrated to the new conditions prevailing in the body of Christ without inordinate difficulty.

Cyril taught people preparing for baptism in fourth century Jerusalem that when "Joshua son of Nun was filled with the spirit of wisdom because Moses had laid his hands on him" (Deut. 34:9), "it was not Moses who bestowed the gift, but the Spirit. . . . In the days of Moses, the Spirit was given by laying on of hands, and by laying on of hands Peter also gives the Spirit. And on thee also who are about to be baptized, shall His grace come; yet in what manner I say not, for I will not anticipate the proper season" (Cyril of Jerusalem, Catech. Lect. XVI.25,26, NPNF 2 VII, p. 122). The grace of baptism brings the believer into this apostolic community ready in any moment or season, now or later, to receive the Spirit. This interpretation leaves room both for explicit theories of baptismal regeneration and of subsequent regenerative renewal after baptism.

# The Duty of Obedience to Apostolic Discipline

To the elders of Pontus, Galatia, and Cappadocia, Peter's First Letter appealed to "be submissive" to duly authorized leadership: "clothe yourselves with humility" because "God opposes the proud but gives grace to the humble" (1 Pet. 5:5). He appealed "as a fellow elder, a witness of Christ's sufferings" that all elders "be shepherds of God's flock that is under your care, serving as overseers—not because you must, but because you are willing," being "eager to serve; not lording it over those entrusted to you, but being examples to the flock" (1 Pet. 5:1–3).

It was expected that discipline and order would prevail in the early Christian community, that leaders would be respected, and that their efforts would lead the faithful to union with Christ (Clement of Rome, Cor. 1.3; 2.8; 4.6–8; AF, pp. 18–20; cf. Gregory I, Hom. on Gospels, II.26, 5, 6). It was "in the apostle's doctrine and fellowship" that the church continued steadfastly after Pentecost (Acts 2:42 KJV).

The Spirit who enables the whole church to live is present and active so as to unite its most distant congregations, its most unique individuals. The local assembly derives its mission through its organic connection with the Vine with its many branches. There would be no localized church were it not for the apostolic mission of the church universal, its revealed Word, its ministry, its holy writ, and missional task (William Tyndale, The Obedience of a Christian Man).

The apostles commended an office of caring, guiding, and ordering through the *episkopos* (overseer or bishop), a caring analogous to judicious parenting, for "if anyone does not know how to manage his own family, how can he take care of God's church?" (1 Tim. 3:5). "Obey your leaders and submit to their authority. They keep watch over you as men who must give an account. Obey them so that their work will be a joy, not a burden" (Heb. 13:17).

In no decade of the last half of the first century does the church appear or proceed without gifted leadership, ordered arrangement, and structured organization. Those who reject the structure of the church altogether reject the inviter, Christ. The offices of the church are the intended instruments by which the Spirit works, yet the Spirit is not limited or bound by these instruments (John 3:8).

# Development of the Apostolic Tradition of Corrective Ministry

In this way the development of apostolic ministry proceeded through at least four successive stages, from Jesus' own ministry, to his instituting and commissioning of a continuing ministry of apostolic traditioning, to the implementation of apostolic ministry in the organization of churches, and finally to a more formally constituted threefold ministry, episcopally ordered, and intergenerationally transmitted.

The details of the first three stages are somewhat obscure. Their treatment by modern interpreters is often colored and beveled by varied vantage points of the interpreters and tilted by extensive traditional memories of interpretation. Already within the period of the writing of the New Testament, the teaching of a threefold ministry was being preliminarily tested and unfolded. The orders of ministry that appeared embryonically in the New Testament were soon to be firmed up in a gradually developing history (Luther, LW 38:186ff.).

The earliest catalogues of offices were later recast in various ways, but gradually took on a relatively stable form. Provisional adjustments were transmuted into more permanent forms of order. Some designated offices appear to belong primarily to the earliest period of Christian history, while others have remained as durable features of the order of the developing body. Resident ministries, as distinguished from previous itinerant missional ministries, appear as early as the Pastoral Letters and the Didache.

# Orders of Apostolic Discipline by the End of the Apostolic Age

By the end of the first century and probably earlier, there is growing clarity from diverse sources about a more firmly developed ministry of *episkopos, presbyteros,* and *diakonos.* Oversight and ordination were ordinarily exercised by *episkopoi* (bishops). Ordinations by *presbyteroi* apart from an *episkopos* were in time regarded as irregular. Apostolic authority was consensually believed to be "transmitted exclusively by devolution, through unbroken episcopal succession from the Apostles, and through them from Christ Himself" (Hall, DT VIII, p. 135; cf. G. Burnet, Of the Pastoral Care, pp. 44–49; C.S. Grüber, Holy Order, pp. 6–66; C. Gore, C&M, Ch. 3; D. Stone, EVO, pp. 41–58).

Clement of Rome argued in the last decade of the first century that Christ himself was providing oversight of the churches through the *episkopoi* (Corinth. 41–44), who if they should "fall asleep, other approved men should succeed to their ministration" (Corinth. 42). Ignatius of Antioch, around 115 A.D., viewed it as an already firmly established tradition that the ministry of bishops, presbyters, and deacons was essential to the church, and distinctly representative of Christ and the Apostles (Eph. 3–6; Magn. 6,7; Trall. 3; Phil. 3–4). According to Ignatius, the bishop appears to be head of a jurisdiction of presbyters who gathered in council as elder advisors and deacons to the bishop (Ignatius, Ephesians, ANF I, pp. 50f., Trallians, pp. 67–69). The unity of diverse elements in the church was insured by the episcopacy as guarantor of unity (Ignatius, Smyrn. 8).

A generation later these patterns of ministry were too widely acknowledged and revered to be imagined as recent achievements. Irenaeus viewed the *episkopos* as by long tradition a local resident leader of a city or area surrounding a city. By the end of the second century there were varied representative writers attesting to lists of bishops connected in unbroken succession with the apostles, who had charged them with guarding the apostolic tradition and administering the eucharist and exercising discipline in the church (Irenaeus, Ag. Her. III.3.1–3; IV.26.2,5; 33.8; Tertullian, Prescript. 32, 36). The line from bishop to bishop was carefully traced and maintained from the earliest time in a given location (Eusebius, CH IV.22.1–4, NPNF 2 I, pp. 198–99). The transition was patterned after Moses who "took of the Spirit that was on him and put the Spirit on the seventy elders. When the Spirit rested on them, they prophesied" (Num. 11:25).

This made the *episkopos* not only the symbol of unity, but also of continuity with tradition (Cyprian, Treatises, I, ANF V, pp. 421–23; John Chrysostom, Hom. on the Statues, NPNF 1 IX, pp. 355–56). The constitutive factor in defining the office of bishop was to stand in a line of succession with the apostles (Hegesippus, Fragments, ANF VIII, pp. 764). Elaborate lists of bishops were carefully assembled to show this continuity (Tertullian, Prescript. Ag. Her., 21–39, ANF III, pp. 252–62; Augustine, Letter, To Generosus, FEF III, 1418, p. 2). Irenaeus appealed to "that tradition which derives from the Apostles, and which is preserved in the churches by the successions of presbyters" (Ag. Her., III.2, ECF, p. 90). The ministry that emerged in the century following Pentecost is "rightly to be accepted as the normative ministry of the Christian Church. It has an *a priori* claim upon us for our acceptance as the proper ministry of the church, just as the faith which was stated at Nicaea and Chalcedon, the worship which became regularized at a much earlier period than that, and the understanding of the meaning of the new life in Christ which flowered during the Roman empire's persecutions of the church, have their *a priori* claim upon those who would be in the mainstream of historical Christian development" (Pittenger, CMR, p. 46).

Cyprian ordained readers and subdeacons. As generations proceeded, various offices emerged in response to various needs, among them, "archdeacons, subdeacons, acolytes. . . exorcists, catechists, singers, doorkeepers, the *copiatae* or *fossarii*, who had care of funerals, the *parabolani*, who took care of the sick, the *defensores* and *oeconomi*, a kind of churchwarden, of which the first took care of land and houses, the latter of money appropriated to charitable uses" (Doddridge, Works, 2:341; cf. P. King, Primitive Church, I.5, sec. 2,3).

Ordained ministers in Protestantism are variously "called *bishops* or *elders*, from the oversight they are to take, and from the grave and prudent example they are to set; *pastors*, from the spiritual food they are to administer; *ministers*, from the service they are to render; *watchmen*, from the vigilance they are to exercise; *teachers*, from the instructions they are to give; *ambassadors*, from the treaty of reconciliation and peace they are sent to effect" (Binney, TCI, p. 188).

# Interlude: A Case of Chronic Pedophilia

I am going to propose another case study for reflection, hoping that these issues can be brought closer to the arena of disciplinary practice.

Pastor Matthew Otis is a fascinating preacher, but a hopeless pedophile. He is removed to another parish, where he returns predictably to pedophilic activity. He is moved to another parish. This happens six times. After the seventh time he is charged by eleven former acolytes with sexual abuse and conduct unbecoming to a minister and brought to civil court with extensive evidence of pedophilial abuse. On the assumption that the evidence is overwhelmingly against the pastor, should the diocese pay reparations? Whose penitence is more pertinent, Pastor Otis' or the church's?

# Recapitulation

The apostolic tradition of admonition awaits retrieval in the postmodern setting. Intrinsic to the Spirit's work of corrective love is the development of an ordered apostolic ministry. The mission of the apostolate is defined by the Lord himself in his Great Commission: to proclaim the Gospel to the world, to teach, to make disciples, and to baptize in the triune name. The time of the apostolate is the entire history between Pentecost and Parousia. Only by adaptably responding to changing historical challenges is the mission of the one, holy, catholic apostolate actualized.

The ordered ministry was founded by Jesus himself in his training of the Twelve for proclamation, teaching, discipling, and the ordering of time through worship. It was from the synagogue that the early Christian *ekklēsia* derived its basic models of discipline and admonition. The synagogue eldership was reshaped into the church's office of *presbyter*. All who voluntarily share in the body of Christ implicitly are by their confirmation of their baptism giving assent to apostolic teaching, and placing themselves under the discipline of an ordered ministry. Although the offices of ministry went through much historical development, that development is organically grounded in the personal relation between Jesus and his disciples. By the end of the apostolic age, the orders of ministry were generally sufficiently fixed and defined to be able to transmute amid new historical challenges without losing their primary identity as defined in the New Testament.

# 9

# How Corrective Love Works through Serving, Teaching, and Superintending Ministries

In what ways does Christ present himself ever anew to the world today as lowly servant (through helping ministries —*diakonos*)? As proclaimer of the truth (through ministries of teaching and guidance—*presbyteros*)? As head of the redeemed body (through the ministry of oversight—*episkopos*)? How are Christ's prophetic, priestly and governing ministries continuing to work correctively within the body of Christ? Is grace present in the setting aside of persons for representative ministry? What effectively occurs in the service of ordination? Does the authorization to sacred orders rest upon Jesus' own intention and specific directive?

## *Diakonos*: The Helping Ministry

It is indicative of their sharing in the humble serving ministry of Jesus that the apostles took no higher title than that of ministers or servants (Col. 1:24–25; Longer Catech., Eastern Orthodox Church, 259, COC II, p. 485). The frame of reference for admonition is loving service. No act of correction is plausible if it betrays a lack of rootage in God's own serving ministry. Admonition comes out of the heart of love.

Jesus' ministry was "unto death" as a ransom (*lutron*) that many might be delivered from spiritual death (Matt. 20:19; Mark 10:45). Our ministry shares in that same servant ministry of God the Son for us, even to the extent of its readiness for death, if need be, in order to attest his saving work, and to participate in his deliverance of sinners from moral and spiritual dissolution (Calvin, Inst. 4.5.15–16).

It is significant that the word most frequently used to describe the ministry of the whole people of God is a word that carried no nuances of authority, dominion, rule, power, prominence, or dignity, but precisely the opposite: service (*diakonia*). The actions of the diaconate share in the Lord's own self-abasement: waiting on tables, serving food, pouring wine, feeding the hungry.

The church is not to follow the pattern of lording it over others: "Instead, the greatest among you should be like the youngest, and the one who rules like the one who serves. For who is greater, the one who is at the table or the one who serves? Is not the one who is at the table? But I am among you as one who serves" (Luke 22:26–27). The very words chosen to describe this unpretentious activity disavow rulership and acquisition of power (Mark 9:33–35; 10:43–5). "But you are not to be called 'Rabbi,' for you have only one Master and you are all brothers. And do not call anyone on earth 'father,' for you have one Father, and he is in heaven. Nor are you to be called 'teacher,' for you have one Teacher, the Christ. The greatest among you will be your servant" (Matt. 23:8–11). Among acts of *diakonia* are collecting and distributing money for the poor (2 Cor. 8:1–6; Rom. 15:25; Acts 11:29–30), acts of personal help and assistance when needed (Acts 19:22; Philem. 13; 2 Tim. 1:18), and the works of love (1 Cor. 13; 16:15).

The *diakonoi* engage in serving ministries that manifest the living Christ in the world. The diaconate is the ministry of service (Polycarp, Phil. 5,2; Didache, 15, 1; Ignatius, Trallians, 2, 3; Apost. Const., II.4.29-32; II.6.41; II.7.44; ANF VII, pp. 410–11, 416, 412; CMM, p. 210–13). The charismatic center and energy of the diaconate is seen in the fact that *diakonia* is rooted in *charisma*: "There are different kinds of gifts, but the same Spirit" so that "to each one the manifestation of the Spirit is given for the common good" (1 Cor. 12:4, 7). "Each one should use whatever gift he has received to serve others" (1 Pet. 4:10; Francis of Assisi, Admonitions,

CWS, pp. 29–35).

"The diaconate is not to be considered as a mere step towards the priesthood, but it is so adorned with its own indelible character and its own special grace that those who are called to it 'can permanently serve the mysteries of Christ and the Church'" (Doc. Vat. II, Diac; CMM, p. 211).

## *Presbyteros*: The Ministry of Teaching and Guidance

The apostolic tradition is preserved unaltered and passed along faithfully to the local congregation through the office of elder or *presbyteros*. In the New Testament, elders (*presbyteroi*) were appointed in every city (Titus 1:5), "in each church" (Acts 14:23) to guide the church and oversee the flock, attentive to its organic relation with the whole body of Christ. *Presbyteros* translates the Hebrew term for the elder who presided over the synagogue, the senior congregational spiritual advisor whose primary functions were faithful teaching and guidance (Calvin, Inst. 4.4,5). It is through the office of *presbyteros* that corrective love takes its most personal focus in the body of Christ.

Two principal presbyteral functions were referred to jointly as the work of "pastors and teachers" (Eph. 4:11; cf. 1 Cor. 12:28; Rom. 12:8; Heb. 13:7, 17; Titus 1:5–9). Elders had a task of directing or guiding the disciplined community in a locale. "The elders who direct the affairs of the church well are worthy of double honor, especially those whose work is preaching and teaching" (1 Tim. 5:17).

In his First Apology (ANF I, pp. 185–86) Justin Martyr gives us an intriguing window into the early Christian service of worship in describing the *presbyteros* as a presiding officer or president of the assembly who stood up and gave spiritual instruction and moral exhortation, after which all the people stood up for prayer, before receiving the bread and wine, and water, the people giving their consent by saying Amen. This picture shows us how the functions of

153

eldership were being exercised in the second century.

The personal agent of admonition in the disciplined community is ordinarily the elder, or if not directly through the elder, it occurs under the care of the elder. In this way the work of corrective love is bound up with the ministry of Word and Sacrament. No act of corrective love is rightly to be detached from the Lord's table and the preached word. If lay counselors mediate this admonition, they do it under the direction of an elder. Due to this liturgical and pedagogical context, pastoral admonition differs from secular psychotherapy.

The spiritual gift which *presbyteroi* receive at their ordination prepares them "not for a sort of limited and narrow mission, but for the widest possible and universal mission of salvation" (Doc. Vat. II, Priest 10, CMM, pp. 200–201) even "to the ends of the earth" (Acts 1:8).

## *Episkopos*: The Ministry of Oversight

The chief shepherd of the flock in a given locale, the overseer or *episkopos* or bishop, is the principle teacher and defender of the faith, the symbolic focus of apostolic authority, and according to Ignatius, the indispensable condition of the existence of the apostolate in a particular place. Without apostolic oversight, "neither Church nor Christian could either be or be spoken of" (Conf. of Dositheus, X, CC, p. 492).

The due administration of the Lord's Supper occurs under the jurisdiction of one who stands in the tradition (variously viewed either manually and linearly by some or symbolically and confessionally by others) of the first apostles. "Let that eucharist be considered valid which is under the bishop or him to whom he commits it" (Ignatius, Smyrna, 8, ANF I, p. 89, NE, p. 28). Any act of admonition that has become severed from this apostolic frame of reference can hardly be called an evangelical admonition in good order.

*Episkopoi* are to be consulted in matters in dispute. The

Canons of Sardica, A.D. 343, held that "a bishop should lend his support to those oppressed by some injustice, or if a widow is afflicted, or a minor despoiled of property—yet he should intercede for these classes only when they seek redress in a just cause" (CCC, p. 21). The right to ordain has normatively been assigned to the *episkopos*, since the grace of ordination brings the ordinand into a solemn covenant to transmit and preserve the apostolic tradition (Apostolic Constitutions, III.I.11, ANF VII, pp. 429–30).

Under conditions of persecution, the compelling reason for being attentive to these overseers was that they represented a cohesive and reliable transmission of the apostolic witness, as distinguished from the centrifugal forces of gnosticism and heresy (Ignatius, Tral. 7; Phil. 2.3.4; Smyrn. 9.1). The conscience of each individual believer was instructed by humbly being attentive to the voice of the whole church and the due representative of the primitive apostolate in that jurisdiction.

"Be subject to the *episkopos* and to one another" (Ignatius, Magn. 13.1,2). The life of humble service is best understood in the context of the life of the crucified Lord of glory whose ministry the *episkopoi* are pledged to transmit. Mutually disposable submission to other's claims and needs is framed in the community of disposability enlivened by the servant Messiah.

The eucharist was offered or caused to be offered under the direction of the *episkopos*. "It is not allowed without the bishop to baptize or hold the Agape, but whatsoever he shall approve, that is also well-pleasing to God, in order that whatsoever is done may be safe and secure" (Ignatius, Smyrna, 8.1, SHD, p. 68; cf. Anon., On the Twelve Apostles, ANF V, p. 255; The Apostolic Tradition of Hippolytus, 2, 3). Only by this unifying order would the church be assured that it is "breaking the one bread, which is the medicine of immortality" (Ignatius, Ephesians 20.2, ANF I, p. 57).

*Episkopoi* offer admonition and guidance which, since it is presumed to be reliably grounded in the earliest apostolic teaching, is eagerly sought and gratefully received by the faithful (Ignatius, Philip., ANF I, p. 79; Apost. Const., II. ANF VII, pp. 496–531). That bishops may err is evident from Augustine's letters to Petilian, where he argued that one should not obey even regularly elected bishops if they teach contrary to Scripture (NPNF 1 IV, 519ff.; cf. Augustine, On Baptism, VII, NPNF 1 IV, pp. 499–514; Augsburg Conf., CC, p. 100).

## Complementary of Orders and Polity Types

From one person to another, God reaches out to communicate love, to illuminate and perfect. The diaconate seeks to love primarily through service, the eldership seeks to teach, admonish, and illumine rightly through the proclaimed word and ordering of the sacramental life, and the episcopate seeks to perfect the whole through protecting the authenticity and transmission of the Sacraments (Dionysius Areopag., coel. hier., 5.1.5,6; 6.3.5; Tho. Aq., ST Suppl., Q37, III, pp. 2689–94). These three grades or orders of ministry have continued without interruption, yet with much development, since the time of the Pastoral Epistles and Luke's account in Acts. "Without these," argued Ignatius, "it is not called a church" (Tral. 3.1; cf. 2.2; 13.2; Eph. 2.2; 20.2).

Though it did not take long for a distinction to arise between *episkopos* and *presbyteros*, it is probable that they were used for a time more or less interchangeably. For Paul instructed Titus to ordain elders in every city, and then turns immediately to say: "A bishop must be blameless." One gets the impression that he might be speaking of the same office in two different terms. Timothy was called to stir up the gifts he had been given in the laying on of hands by the presbyters (1 Tim. 4:14).

The first letter of Peter concluded by addressing "the elders among you." The writer appealed to his readers as "a fellow *elder*, a witness of Christ's sufferings and one who also will share in the glory to be revealed," hoping that these elders would "be shepherds of God's flock that is under your care, serving as *overseers*," in relation to the expected coming of "the Chief Shepherd" (1 Pet. 5:1–4, italics added).

Despite these incidental usages, in Paul's letter to Philippi *episkopos* and *presbyteros* appear to be distinguishable (Phil. 1:1; cf. Eph. 3; Chrysostom, Homilies to Phil. 1; Ignatius, Trallians 3; Eusebius on Ps. 9,14; Theodoret on 1 Tim. 3:1). However unclear their earlier relationship, it became generally acknowledged by the end of the first century that the distinction between bishop and presbyter could serve a useful function, assuming the premise of Christian freedom to order disciplinary matters usefully and expeditiously.

The vast historical experience of Christianity with church governance should be studied and listened to in making present polity and administrative decisions. That experience generally points toward a consultative, caring, procedurally fair, deliberative type of governance, with corrective love working to heal the corruptions of the church. The Spirit governs the church more effectively through persuasion, free inquiry, voluntary discipline, and due process than by manipulative, pretentious, or coercive attitudes.

From the fifth century onward, the ordinand has commonly received certain insignia of ordination. In the eastern rite, *diakonoi* received the insignia of diaconal office: the orarion (deacon's stole), the maniples (a silk band worn hanging over the left forearm as a eucharistic vestment), and the sacramental fan (to winnow grain from chaff); *presbyteroi* upon being ordained received the stole, the band or girdle, the chasuble, and the prayerbook; and *episkopoi*, upon being consecrated, received insignia proper to their office: the dalmatic (a wide-sleeved senatorial vestment worn under the chasuble), the omophorion or pallium (cloak or mantle), the pectoral cross, the mitre (headdress), and the crosier (shepherding staff).

While some traditions tend to emphasize *presbyteral* consultation with oversight leadership so as to engender lay support, other traditions have focussed more on *serving lay mission* requiring overseeing leadership through presbyteral nurture, while others focus on the continuity of *episcopal* presence to order the whole. From these strains there have come three competing tendencies in theories of church governance: Episcopal governance holds that the power of ordination is reserved for the bishop exclusively. Presbyteral governance holds that there is one order of ministers—elders—having equal rights and prerogatives, over whom there is no higher authority. Congregational governance holds that the congregation itself ordains and governs according to Scripture (for classic statements of these views see the letters of Ignatius and Cyprian, Calvin, Inst. 4.3–5; Thirty-Nine Articles, XXXIV, CC, pp. 277–78; Hooker, LEP IV:1; Dale, Manual of Congregational Principles). These may be understood historically as complementary types that each have had their day, and today need to be fittingly melded (for a promising model of such melding, see BEM).

Several elders joined together constituted a synod of elders or *coetus presbyterorum* entrusted to undertake certain duties (Cyprian, Letters, V, IX, XI, ANF V, pp. 283, 290, 292). It may have occurred that this collegium of elders led to the appointment of one to preside over them, who came to be called *episkopos*, since the task of overseeing the larger community would have fallen upon him. Jerome argued that at an early date the churches were governed by the conjoint counsel of presbyters, and that afterward it became a universal expedient that one of these elders should be chosen as chief shepherd of the church of an area: "a presbyter is the same as a bishop, and before ambition came into religion. . . the churches were governed by the direction of presbyters, acting as a body" (Jerome, Comm. on Titus, LCF, p. 189; cf. Letters, NPNF 2 VI, p. 288; Second Helvetic Conf., CC, p. 158; Calvin, Inst. 4.11.6). Jerome reminded bishops that they held an office strongly shaped by common custom, and probably conditioned by the consent of the elders.

Aside from Jerome's view that the episcopacy evolved from the presbyterate, the broader consensus of the ancient ecumenical writers was that the episcopacy was of apostolic if not dominical origin (a point that Jerome elsewhere also affirms). Overseers were collegially equal, but certain bishops of important cities were by tradition designated as metropolitans or patriarchs, to whom the surrounding dioceses looked for spiritual guidance and apostolic fidelity.

## The Whole *Laos* Shares in the Grace of Christ's Prophetic, Priestly, and Governance Ministries

Every member of the body shares in the prophetic, priestly, and governance mission of the Son, there being only one priesthood (Christ's), one teaching office (Christ's), and one office of governance (Christ's), in which each member participates by faith active in love (Russian Catechism, COC II, p. 466; Ursinus, CHC, pp. 170–76; Doc. Vat. II, Ch 33).

The whole body of Christ duly takes part in his *prophetic* ministry. For laity as well as clergy witness to the Gospel, and some, both women and men, old and young, are given gifts of prophetic vision. Evangelization is a task of the whole body. The Spirit is being poured out on "all people," so that "your sons and daughters will prophesy, your young men will see visions, your old men will dream dreams. Even on my servants, both men and women, I will pour out my Spirit in those days, and they will prophesy" (Acts 2:17–18; Joel 2:28–29). The laity are on the front line of the struggle against the world-rulers of darkness, against spiritual forces of wickedness (Eph. 3:10, 6:12; Doc. Vat. II, Ch 35, p. 61). Through their families, vocations, friendships, and networks of communication, they bear living testimony to God's mercy and justice (Luther, LW 26:16–21, 27:119ff.; Congar, Lay People in the Church).

The whole body of Christ duly shares in his *priestly* ministry. All the people offer their praise to God's glory, and their service within the passing *saeculum* in their precise vocational locality. As such, every member of the spiritual priesthood of Christ is called to some significant vocation in the world, to serve God by service to the neighbor (Luther,

LW 31:353–56, 39:227–36). Every aspect of daily life becomes a sacrificial offering, so that "you also, like living stones, are being built into a spiritual house to be a holy priesthood, offering spiritual sacrifices acceptable to God through Jesus Christ" (1 Pet. 2:4–5). It is the bread and wine harvested by the laity that is symbolically offered and presented in the Eucharist. The laity thus share in the consecration of the whole world to God (Luther, Comm. on Ps. 110, LW 13, p. 331; Doc. Vat. II, Ch 34).

The whole body of Christ duly shares in his ministry of *governance* and consummation, for all things ultimately will be subject to the Son as the Son is subject to the Father (Phil. 3:21; 1 Cor. 15:26–28; Doc. Vat. II, Ch 36, p. 62–63). Christ is overcoming the power of the Enemy, binding up the strong man—sin. All the members of the body of Christ are privileged to share in that emergent victory, so as to be enabled by grace to conquer sin in themselves (Rom. 6:12). It is to the people of God that the promise is made: "All things are yours," whether in "life or death or the present or the future—all are yours, and you are of Christ, and Christ is of God" (1 Cor. 3:21–23).

In history it has often been *laos* rather than *klēros*, who have rescued the church from corruption. When the laity following the missioners of Francis Xavier in Japan were deprived of all clergy and completely cut off from connection with the mothering church, the faithful *laos*, even without the written word or eucharist, armed only with their baptism, and their memory of Scripture and tradition, even threatened by horrible persecutions, kept the faith alive in Japan for two centuries. Similarly in China during the Cultural Revolution, the church remained quietly alive, amid persecution, in the hearts of believers. The vitality of Russian Christianity after 73 years of relentless oppression attests to the vitality of the faith of the laity. Church history abounds with such witnesses, even under diabolical police states.

Hilary of Poitiers, himself a bishop, had the grace to recognize that "the ears of the people are more holy than the hearts of the bishops" (quoted in Moss, The Christian Faith, p. 227; cf. Trin., VIII.1, NPNF 2 IX, p. 137).

# Whether the Ministry of Reconciliation Is Rightly Termed a Priesthood

James clearly refers to praying for forgiveness as a duty deliberately assigned to elders: "Is any one of you in trouble? He should pray. Is anyone happy? Let him sing songs of praise. Is any one of you sick? He should *call the elders* of the church to pray over him and anoint him with oil in the name of the Lord. And the prayer offered in faith will make the sick person well; the Lord will raise him up. If he has sinned, he will be forgiven. Therefore confess your sins to each other and pray for each other so that you may be healed. The prayer of a righteous man is powerful and effective" (James 5:13–16). The *presbyteroi* have this task attached to their office. They perform the apostolic function of mediating and making effective the healing and forgiving ministry of Christ himself (C&S, 35).

Paul understood himself to be "a minister of Christ Jesus to the Gentiles with the priestly duty (*hierourgounta*) of proclaiming the gospel of God, so that the Gentiles might become an offering (*prosphara*) acceptable to God, sanctified (*hēgiasmenē*) by the Holy Spirit" (Rom. 15:16; cf. John Chrysostom, On the Priesthood, NPNF 1 IX, pp. 40–47). Four times in that passage Paul used images from the priestly tradition to describe his ministry.

At Jerusalem the number of disciples "increased rapidly, and a large number of priests became obedient to the faith" (Acts 6:7). As long as former Jewish priests were in the Jerusalem or other churches it might have caused needless confusion to call apostolic ministers priests (Gk: *heireus*, priest; Lat: *sacerdos*). The English word priest is derived from the shortening of *presbyteros*, as is the French *pretre* and Italian *prete* (cf. Spanish *presbitero*). Yet the Greek *presbyteros* has somewhat different connotations than the

Hebrew words for "priest" (*kohen*, Gk: *hiereus*). By the time of Cyprian the priestly metaphors of the Old Testament had been transferred to the term and functions of the *presbyteros* (Lightfoot, Comm. on Philippians, pp. 242–66). Soon *episkopos*, *presbyteros*, and *diakonos* would be viewed as broadly analogous to the Jewish high priests, priests and Levites (Apostolic Constitutions, II, ANF VII, pp. 396–414).

The first reference to the distinction between a layperson (*laikos*) and clergy is found very early in Clement of Rome, who was applying the regulations of Leviticus to Christian worship: "The high priest has been given his own special services, the priests have been assigned their own place, and the Levites have their special ministrations enjoined on them. The layman is bound by the ordinances of the laity" (Corinth, 40, ECF, p. 32). The *presbyteroi* administered the eucharist and offer prayers representatively for the whole church.

## Christ's Priesthood and Ours

While Jesus did not describe himself or his disciples as priests, the community who remembered him described his death in terms of sacrificial images, his cross as a sacrificial death, and himself as both lamb and high priest. Christ offered his life as an expiatory sacrifice for the sins of the world (John Chrysostom, On the Priesthood, NPNF 1 IX, pp. 75–79; Ambrose, Of the Christian Faith, NPNF 2 X, p. 255).

The New Testament thus speaks of the priesthood of Jesus Christ (Heb. 4:14), and of the priesthood of the whole people of God who share by faith in his body (1 Peter 2:5–9; Rev. 1:6; Luther, Retraction, LW 39, pp. 229–38). Protestants have commonly made this sort of distinction: "The apostles of Christ do term all those who believe in Christ 'priests,' not in regard to their ministry, but because that all the faithful, being made kings and priests, may, through Christ, offer up spiritual sacrifices unto God" (Second Helvetic Conf., CC, p. 154; 1 Pet. 2:5–9; Rev. 1:6).

The spiritual priesthood of all believers offers eucharistic sacrifice of prayer, praise, thanksgiving, and oblation to the service of God. Only Jesus Christ is sacrificing priest, being both priest and sacrifice. The Christian minister is a priest in the same sense that all believers are priests, yet he acts representatively for all believers (Luther, Pagan Servitude of the Church, MLS pp. 347–49; An Appeal to the Ruling Class, pp. 407–8; Jacobs, SCF, pp. 422–23). This ministry is representative of all the members of the church who constitute a "holy priesthood" (1 Pet. 2:5), appointed by one who is still "a priest forever, in the order of Melchizedek" (Heb. 5:6). "The minister discharges a priestly office as the representative of his fellow-members of the universal priesthood of believers. . . yet his authority to minister the Word and Sacraments is not derived from them, but from Him who called him to be an ambassador" (Hughes, CF, p. 195).

In Luther's view, the ministerial office rests úpon the priesthood of all believers. To the whole church is given the office of the keys, of administering the Sacraments and preaching and discipline. But not all can preach, and even if they could, there would be great confusion if all should simultaneously wish to exercise shepherding and teaching functions. Hence "the individual members of the congregation agree to transfer their rights to one whom they call and who now acts in their place," hence ordination is viewed as "the confirmation of the act of transferring in an individual charge the office of the ministry by the many priests to the one" (Neve, Luth. Sym., pp. 234–36; cf. Calvin, Inst. 4.17–19).

Christ did not become a priest by taking the role upon himself, but through the Father's appointment (Heb. 5:4–6). His priesthood is not Levitically inherited or from the order of Aaron, but from the higher order of Melchizedek (Heb. 7:1–28). Sinners in the Mosaic covenant are unable rightly to offer sacrifice, hence are duly represented by the priest. So are the new people of God unable to come before God unless represented by the Son who is the lamb, who shares their frame and understands their humanity (Heb. 5:1–3).

Unlike temple sacrifice which was daily and seasonally

renewed, Jesus' unique, single sacrifice is once for all offered on the cross, needing no renewal, as priest forever, setting the former commandment aside (Heb. 7:15–18; 9:24–28; 10:10–19; Küng, The Church, pp. 36-47). "Jesus suffered outside the city gate to make the people holy through his own blood. Let us, then, go to him outside the camp, bearing the disgrace he bore" (Heb. 13:12–13). All who live in union with Christ who suffered outside the gate will go to meet him outside the camp, leaving the old cultus—a perfect priesthood replacing all previous priests.

It is the whole people of God who are from the outset called to be a kingdom of priests: "Although the whole earth is mine, you will be for me a kingdom of priests and a holy nation" (Ex. 19:5–6). "For you are a people holy to the LORD your God. The LORD your God has chosen you out of all the peoples on the face of the earth to be his people" (Deut. 7:6). Similarly in the body of Christ, all who live in union with Christ share in his holiness, and receive the indwelling Spirit. The faithful living stones "are being built into a spiritual house to be a holy priesthood (heirateuma hagion), offering spiritual sacrifices acceptable to God through Jesus Christ" (1 Pet. 2:5)—a temple of the Holy Spirit, enlivened by the Spirit.

That a time should be set apart to honor God is a requirement of the law of nature grasped universally by natural moral reasoning. So in the revealed Word, God has appointed "one day in seven for a Sabbath, to be kept holy unto him; which, from the beginning of the world to the resurrection of Christ was the last day of the week; and from the resurrection of Christ, was changed into the first day of the week, which in Scripture is called the Lord's day," in which all are to "observe an holy rest all the day from their own works, words, and thoughts" (Westminster Conf., CC, p. 218).

# Prophetic, Priestly, and Guiding Aspects of the Ministry of Corrective Love

Since Christ is the anointed messianic type of prophet, priest, and Davidic shepherd-king, Christ's ministry is derivatively prophetic, priestly, and protectively-guiding. The three duties of the representative ministry (to proclaim the Word, administer the Sacraments, and govern the church by pastoral care and good discipline), correspond with the threefold mission of Christ as prophet, priest, and shepherd-king (Oden,WL, ch. 9. 14). The church by its commission and essential definition has a teaching ministry, a ministry of Sacraments, and a ministry of care of souls. The classic Protestant text setting forth this threefold authorization is "to preach the Gospel, to forgive and retain sins, and to administer and distribute the Sacraments" (Augsburg Conf., CC p. 98).

# Prophetic Ministry as Teaching the Word with Authority

The prophetic office of Christ, and therefore derivatively of his Church and ministry, is to preach and teach the Word. The prophetic office of the church and its representative ministry occurs by Christ's direction and commission to "make disciples of all nations, baptizing them . . . [and] teaching them to obey everything I have commanded you" (Matt. 28:19–20; cf. Mark 16:15). Jesus said of the apostolate: "He who receives you receives me, and he who receives me receives the one who sent me" (Matt. 10:40). Preaching as a public act in common worship remains a duty, calling, and prerogative of ordered ministry.

The entire body functions prophetically as the whole people (*laos*), yet the prophetic office is representatively performed through a duly called sacred ministry. All members share in the apostolate by support and consent (Tertullian, Exhortation, VII, ANF IV, p. 54). Ordained

165

ministers share in this prophetic ministry by their calling, preparation, ordination, and assignment (Apostolic Constitutions, VIII.II–III, ANF VII, pp. 482, 492ff.; Hugh of St. Victor, SCF, pp. 271ff.).

The prophetic office places upon the whole church the duty of resisting false teachers. The ministries of edification, education, and evangelization all are expressions of the whole church's participation in Christ's prophetic ministry. Ministry upbuilds souls, teaches the truth, and proclaims good news to all.

Attestation of the Gospel in private and unofficial communications apart from common worship is thus the duty of every Christian believer. Paul was addressing the whole church at Colossae when he said, "Let the word of Christ dwell in you richly as you teach and admonish one another with all wisdom, and as you sing psalms, hymns and spiritual songs" (Col. 3:16).

The chief subject of preaching is the Gospel, not the daily newspaper or personal autobiography. Preaching instructs the laity according to Scripture, not according to private opinion or debatable theory or speculative intuition (Luther, Answer to Emser, LW 39, pp. 182–85). Preachers are not authorized to preach just anything that comes to mind, but rather the good news of God's salvation. One does not select sermon topics on the basis of how they will be admired by laity. Paul wrote, "If I were still trying to please men, I would not be a servant of Christ" (Gal. 1:10). If a physician judged his medication by its taste or acceptability to the patient, who would trust him?

## Priestly Ministry as Intercession

The priestly office of Christ, and therefore derivatively of his Church and ministry, is prototypically seen in the celebration of the Sacraments. The priestly office proceeds by Christ's direction and commission to offer God's grace to all humanity so as to enable humanity to draw near to God.

After the Supper Jesus took the cup and said, "This cup is the new covenant in my blood, which is poured out for you" (Luke 22:20). His shed blood accomplished what the blood of animal sacrifice could merely anticipate in the old covenant: atonement of sin, reconciliation of sinners to God, allowing all humanity to draw near to God.

These words from the last Supper were burned into the memories of the apostles: "This cup is the new covenant in my blood" (1 Cor. 11:25). By our eating and drinking this bread and cup we "proclaim the Lord's death until he comes" (1 Cor. 11:26). It is through this eating and drinking that the whole community becomes "a holy priesthood, offering spiritual sacrifices acceptable to God through Jesus Christ" (1 Pet. 2:5). The whole body therefore participates in Christ's own priesthood for the world. There is no individual priesthood in Christianity that stands alone or apart from Christ's priesthood for all. Nonetheless it is exercised representatively by those in the office of sacred ministry of behalf of the whole body.

These actions do not bestow grace without faith or coerce a sanctifying influence apart from freely cooperative responses on the part of the recipient. They do not have unconditional efficacy *ex opere operato*. They offer nothing less than God's own grace to human freedom. Unworthy participation in them is hazardous to one's soul.

The gifts of convicting, justifying, and sanctifying grace are offered through Word and Sacrament. By these means humanity draws near to God on the basis of the eucharistic sacrifice of Christ on our behalf. Leadership in common worship, prayer, petition and intercession, correlates with participation in Christ's priestly ministry.

The presbyter shares in the priestly work of Christ by baptizing penitents into the community of faith, by reconciling baptized penitents who have fallen, by caring for the sick, and by celebrating the Lord's Supper. By all these means the *presbyteroi*, bound together through the *episkopoi*'s ministry of oversight, seek to make Christ present through the apostolic witness in every congregation (Ignatius, Smyrna,

8.1,2; Apost. Const., VIII.3.12–29; ANF VII, pp. 486–94; Doc. Vat. II, Priest 5, Ch 28).

# Ministry of Governance as Guidance and Protection through the Spirit

The regal or gubernatorial or guiding-governing office of Christ, and therefore derivatively of his church and ministry, his spiritual priesthood and apostolate, is to guide and protect the body of Christ, consonant with what is expected of any shepherd-pastor-guide-governor. The guiding-governing office of the church and its representative ministry occurs by Christ's direction, commission, and enabling, in order to guide and protect the faithful until the Lord's return. This guidance role is given to the whole lay apostolate, and is representatively expressed and embodied in sacred ministry.

"It is, I take it, equally wrong and disorderly that all should wish to rule, and that no one should accept" the office of guidance—wrote Gregory the Theologian—nonetheless "I did not nor do I now, think myself qualified to rule a flock or herd, or to have authority over the souls of men." If it is hard to "submit to rule, it seems far harder to know how to rule" over others, and hardest of all to rule oneself (Gregory Nazianzen, Orat. II.4, 9, 10, NPNF 2 VII, pp. 205–207).

# Duties of Sacred Administry

Lay persons do well amid the present dilemma of the blemished church to understand clearly the traditional reasoning underlying ordained ministry. Lacking this groundwork, it may not be entirely clear how much laity have at stake in the revitalization of sacred ministry.

The Second Helvetic Confession astutely sorted out and condensed the duties of ministry in these three categories:

*Teaching of the Gospel* by
    gathering the assembly for worship,
    expounding the Word of God,
    applying doctrine to the current condition of believers,
    educating the unlearned,
    exhorting all to grow at their best pace,
    comforting the fainthearted,
    arming against temptations,
    bringing home those who go astray,
    raising the fallen,
    protecting the flock from wolves, and
    admonishing wisely, not winking at offenses.

*Administration of the Sacraments* by
    commending their right use,
    preparing for their proper reception by wholesome
        teaching,
    maintaining unity of the faithful,
    resisting divisiveness,
    catechizing the ignorant,
    caring for the poor,
    visiting the sick,
    providing for public prayer, and
    securing whatever belongs to the tranquillity, peace,
        and safety the church.

These duties can only be rightly performed
through *discipline* by
    rightly reverencing God,
    praying diligently,
    giving oneself much to the reading of the Scripture,
    being at all times attentive, watchful, and
    showing forth a good example (Second Helvetic Conf.,
        CC, pp. 158–159).

# The Immediate Call of God
# Viewed Experientially

The call to sacred ministry signifies the election and designation of a person for this work of admonition. It comes by means of an inner conviction of responsibility that is awakened by the Holy Spirit in one's heart to serve in the ministry of Word and Sacrament. God the Spirit moves to elicit the awareness of the need for ministry as it relates to one's own gifts and competencies. By this means one is led to the conviction of duty to undertake sacred ministry despite any difficulties that might emerge. The hearer is prepared for recognition of a vocation from God by reading Scripture, and often by conversations with soul friends, parents, pastors, educators, and significant companions.

One who is considering sacred ministry without being in some form credibly called by God and conscience is well advised to think, pray, and study further. For the inward call requires the outward confirmation of the believing community. "No one should publicly teach in the Church or administer the Sacraments, unless he be regularly called" (Augsburg Conf., XIV, CC, p. 72; Chemnitz, MWS, p. 30). No one preaches unless called. No one is called only privately so as to circumvent the consent of the community of faith.

Some have argued that anyone who thinks himself moved by the Spirit should have the right to teach publicly in the church, hence that a general education for public ministry might seem less than necessary, for one only needs the inward sense of being called by the Spirit. Luther remarked wryly: "If all would run together to baptize the child they would drown it" (Neve, Luth. Sym., p. 232). Not all who merely wish to be ministers should be elected, but only such "as are fit and have sufficient learning, especially in the Scriptures, and godly eloquence, and wise simplicity" (Second Helvetic Conf., CC, p. 153). The canons of the Council of Nicea caution: "Neophytes in the faith are not to be ordained to Holy Orders before they have a knowledge of Holy Scriptures" (Nicea I, Ecumenical Councils, NPNF 2

XIV, p. 46).

The point of an ordered call to ministry is not to exclude the laity, but rather to include the laity in the duly received apostolic tradition, and thereby to serve, improve, and enable the laity's ministry by a well-fitted ordained ministry. Lay Christians need the support, challenge, and admonition of godly ministers. They are encouraged to test supposed prophets and teachers (Matt. 7:15–16; 1 Thess. 5:21; 1 John 4:1). The whole *laos* consents to the right calling of one to sacred ministry (Acts 1:23; 6:2–5).

The precise ways in which a call comes may vary widely. The church has been left considerable liberty to be guided by the ordinary operation of the Holy Spirit working through the means of grace under the guidance of Scripture.

# The Calling to Sacred Ministry as Mediated by Due Process through the *Ekklēsia*

The inward or immediate call is that received directly from God. The outward or mediate call is that call received mediately through the church's action in God's name (Luther, Lectures on Galatians, LW 26, pp. 17–18; cf. LW 22, p. 482; Chemnitz, MWS, pp. 31–33).

It is essentially the call of the Son and the giving of the gifts of the Spirit that makes one a minister, not merely the formal rite of ordination as such. Yet for the sake of good order it is fitting not to begin exercising an inward sense of calling until it has been outwardly declared and ratified by the church's confirming action in ordination. All should be forewarned that just because one experiences an apparent inward call, that does not mean that it will necessarily be confirmed by the church outwardly as a regular call. One ought not to presume to undertake duties of ministry solely on the basis of an inward call alone, without outward confirmation by the church, lest one fall into individualistic enthusiasms (Ambrose, Letters, 63, NPNF 2 X, p. 463; Calvin, Inst. 4.3–5).

Some reflective time is ordinarily required for processing, examining, and validating one's sense of calling to sacred ministry (Ignatius Loyola, Spiritual Exercises, pp. 84–87, 104ff.). The disciples accompanied Jesus for three years, all the while not fully understanding their call. It took Paul many years after his initial meeting with the risen Christ before he entered actively into his office of ministry. Although Paul was directly called by the living Lord, nevertheless Ananias was sent to impose his hands, that this call might become rightly manifested to the church (Acts 9:17; Luther, Infiltrating and Clandestine Preachers, LW 40, pp. 386–88; Gerhard, LT, VI, 97; Jacobs, SCF, p. 433).

One normally enters into candidacy for sacred ministry by setting out upon a course of scholastic preparation for ministry, studying Scripture, church history, theology, ethics, and pastoral studies. During this time one remains under the experienced care of those in ministry who will encourage sufficient self-evaluation and vocational assessment that one hopes in due time will confirm the call to ministry (Cyprian, Letters, FC 51, pp. 265ff.). This deliberative process may culminate in ordination.

The confirmed call to ministry carries with it the promise that God the Spirit intends to enable and fulfill that ministry. Whomever God the Son calls, God the Spirit enables (Calvin, Inst. 4.3, 4). If called to danger, it is with God's protection; if to patience, with God's help. When God called Moses and the people of Israel to the desert, they were not left there lacking supply. The sea opened, the heavens yielded manna for survival, the dry earth gave water, their clothing did not wear out, their feet were not bruised, their enemies were overcome. Similarly the seventy-two went out without silver or gold, without purse or staff, yet lacked nothing (Luke 10:1–17). Paul remarked to Corinth's faithful: "So I will very gladly spend for you everything I have and expend myself as well" (2 Cor. 12:15).

In a locale where no effective ministry has yet been provided, where preaching and Sacrament are lacking, under emergency conditions, according to Luther, lay persons may

undertake actions ordinarily reserved for ordained ministers. "If a company of pious Christian laymen were captured
and sent to a desert place, and had not among them an
ordained priest, and were all agreed in the matter, and
elected one and told him to baptize, administer the Mass,
absolve, and preach, such a one would be as true a priest as if
all the bishops and people had ordained him" (Luther, in
Hagenbach, Hist. Doctr., 2, p. 294). "Where there is, therefore,
a true Church, the right to elect and to ordain ministers
necessarily exists. . . Augustine narrates the story of two
Christians in a ship, one of whom baptized the catechumen,
who after baptism, in turn absolved the baptizer"
(Melanchthon, Schmalkald Articles, Appendix, p. 350; cf.
Zoecklerk, Augsburg Conf., p. 246).

## The Grace of Ordination

Ordination is that rite in which the church prays for
ordinands to receive that grace and authority requisite to the
performance of their ministry. Sacramentally viewed, it is
the prayer for and offering of grace for ministry. Formally
viewed, it is the solemn, public testimony and ratification of
the inward call to ministry, the formal induction into office
of one who has been called. "In Orders [one] receives grace
spiritually to regenerate, feed, and nurture others, by
doctrine and Sacraments" (Longer Catech., Eastern Orthodox
Church, 286, COC II, p. 491).

This rite occurs by means of prayer for the Spirit's
enabling, with the laying on of hands (1 Tim. 4:14; 5:22;
2 Tim. 1:6; Luther, Concerning the Ministry, LW 40, pp.
37–40). Hands are laid upon the ordinand to supplicate for
the conveyance of the gifts of sacred ministry, and to reenact,
convey, and symbolize the continuity of apostolic ministry,
even as baptism is accompanied by prayer for the gifts of
baptism.

Traditionally it has been taught that Christ himself
anticipatively instituted ordination by choosing and calling

his apostles by name, and commissioning them to continue his work by ordaining those who would succeed them. It is the Spirit, not the rite itself, that makes persons ordained as overseers and shepherds of the flock which Christ ransomed with his blood (Acts 20:28; Luther, Concerning the Ministry, LW 40, pp. 23–25, 35–36). Like all sanctifying liturgical acts, the rite of ordination is an action of receiving grace with thanksgiving. It recognizes that this person's life, like any good received of God, may be "consecrated by the word of God and prayer" (1 Tim. 4:5).

By whose hand does ordination to sacred ministry occur? On this question there are wide differences between Roman Catholic, Lutheran, Reformed, and charismatic traditions. Catholic, Orthodox, Anglican and other liturgical traditions generally hold that one is ordained only by a bishop in historic apostolic succession, and that a bishop must be consecrated by two or more bishops (Eastern Orthodox Catechism, p. 81). Reformed traditions generally view ordination as administered by the *presbyteroi* (1 Tim. 4:14), assuming that when Paul spoke in 2 Tim. 1:6 of laying on of his own hands, he was one of the presbyters. Congregational and Baptist traditions view ordination as administered by the authority of the *laos*. Some argue that even if the ministry of the laity has the right to ordain, that right should not be exercised if it leads to confusion when asserted. Some hold that one should be ordained to a specific call or work, and not *sine titulo*, or generally to a diffuse apostolate without a specific local calling.

Traditionally it is often said that ministers can be removed from their offices, but not from their orders. Their consecration, according to Catholic teaching, is a sacramental act of an indelible nature, hence irrevocable, as is baptism, even if due to apostasy one might be suspended from ordinal functions.

In the Protestant tradition, many hold that authority conferred may be withdrawn. The Lutheran tradition rejects the doctrine of *character indelibilis* on the grounds that "it is the ministry of the Word that makes a priest or bishop" (Luther, Babylonian Captivity, in SCF, p. 431; cf. Concerning the Ministry, LW 40, p. 35).

In the Catholic tradition, while the power of jurisdiction can be lost, the power of orders is indelible. While one may move from one diocese to another by consent, one does not move from being ordained to being unordained, for ordination is irreversible. Augustine established this point over against the Donatists who argued that one cannot be a minister unless one is exemplary in character, hence if one should neglect moral character, one would entirely cease being duly ordained. Augustine argued that one may lose one's specific appointment in a jurisdiction, but one's ordination is enduring. Jurisdiction is limited to a particular location, while ordination is for service to the whole church. A minister is not authorized to exercise ministerial authority in another parish except by consent.

Paul asked: "How can they hear without someone preaching to them? And how can they preach unless they are sent?" (Rom. 10:14–15). No one is rightly authorized to preach in common worship except as duly called by God and sent on behalf of the whole people. For "No one takes this honor upon himself; he must be called by God, just as Aaron was. So Christ also did not take upon himself the glory of becoming a high priest. But God said to him, 'You are my Son'" (Heb. 5:4–5). This stands in the Mosaic tradition in which representative office is characteristically viewed as responding to the divine initiative rather than presumptively taking human initiative to priesthood and mission (Ex. 28), for Yahweh has "given you the priesthood as a gift" (Num. 18:7).

This is why in common worship no one should ordinarily in the Church "publicly teach or administer the Sacraments without a regular call" (Augsburg Conf., Art. XIV). This allows full freedom for lay persons to teach Scripture studies apart from public worship, engage in serving ministries, lead in congregational life, and assist in common worship. A lay person in times of vacancy or special celebration may serve in the pulpit in sanctuary services assuming that there is a call for such an occasion and that this is a temporary assignment (SCF, p. 430). Further, "When a Christian is among heathen ignorant of the Christian faith, then, according to his ability, he can teach others and propagate Christian doctrine at the promptings of love and necessity. But where a church has been established, let no one, without an ordinary call, undertake the holy office" (Hollaz, in SCD, p. 430).

# On the Necessity of Sacred Ministry

The functions of ministry must neither be depreciated simply because God has the power to work apart from these means, nor overestimated as if primordially essential to God. So who are Apollos and Paul? "Only servants, through whom you came to believe" (1 Cor. 3:5), for it is only God who makes things grow (v. 7). God teaches "by his word, outwardly through his ministers" while moving inwardly to persuade the heart to belief by the Spirit (Second Helvetic Conf., CC, p. 151).

Ministry is not necessary to God to whom no creature is antecedently necessary, yet God wills to provide his gathered people with fit means of guidance, consequent to his will to offer salvation to sinners, hence ministry is considered necessary to the saving purpose of God.

Ministry is not an optional or omissible locus of Christian teaching. The church must have leadership, because its very historically enmeshed being requires intergenerational transmission. It is difficult to imagine a church without some due process for making policy decisions about new historical contingencies. The church does not have the freedom to dispense with leadership.

Some hold that the form of ministry is a wholly secondary issue, hardly of the same order as faith or justification or Sacrament. Others hold that the specific way of ordering ministry is so crucial as to be virtually inseparable from the faith of the church. The distance separating these two views makes ecumenical agreement on ministry difficult.

## Apostolic Authority Derived from Christ

Ministry rests upon Christ's own design, will, and institution. Paul did not hesitate to write to Corinth: "And in the church *God has appointed* first of all apostles, second prophets, third teachers, then workers of miracles, also those having gifts of healing" (1 Cor. 12:28, italics added). Ministry is ordered according to God's own appointment, when authentic, not a culture-bound passing phase or political stratagem or social role that can be reduced to sociological determinants. Christ himself "gave some to be apostles, some to be prophets, some to be evangelists, and some to be pastors and teachers, to prepare God's people for works of service, so that the body of Christ may be built up until we all reach unity in the faith" (Eph. 4:11–13).

The original *apostles* were those immediately commissioned by Christ to attest his resurrection and teach its significance. Those who continue to preserve and renew that apostolate are not properly called apostles, but servants, guides, and overseers of the apostolate.

*Prophets* were persons with gifts of extraordinary grace-enabled judgment and understanding, Spirit-filled individuals who declared and interpreted the Word of God as the Spirit gave them utterance, those especially attentive to the Spirit who were able to bring the historical memory of God's saving action into current application to contemporary hearers (Clementina, Recognitions, I, VIII, ANF VIII, pp. 88–90; 181–82; Homilies, 229–30; 247–48; cf. C. Gore, C&M, Appendix I; D. Stone, Episcopacy and Valid Orders, pp. 6–18).

*Evangelists* were called to constantly renew the apostolate by proclaiming the good news of God's personal coming in Jesus Christ. They set forth the terms of salvation: repentance, faith, and baptism.

A *pastor* is one who shepherds the flock, feeds and nurtures faith, guides the community of believers through hazards to green pastures (Gregory I, Pastoral Care, I.1–3, ACW 11, pp. 21–25) who is called to "feed my sheep" (John 21:16 KJV), keeping "watch over yourselves and all the flock of which the Holy Spirit has made you overseers" (Acts 20:28), as "shepherds of God's flock that is under your care" (1 Pet. 5:2; cf. 2:25; John 10:11; Heb. 13:20; John Chrysostom, Hom. on the Statues, NPNF 1 IX, pp. 354–56, 399; On the Priesthood, II.2, pp. 55–56). Paul addressed the elders at Miletus: "Keep watch over yourselves and all *the flock of which the Holy Spirit has made you overseers.* Be shepherds of the church of God, which he bought with his own blood" (Acts 20:28, italics added; Ignatius, Phil. 2,3, AF, p. 104; Wyclif, The Pastoral Office, II.1, LCC XIV, p. 48).

The *diaconate* is a serving ministry of relief to poor, collecting tithes for distribution to the needy, and serving the worshiping community at prayer and at the Lord's table.

Though some offices may be argued as temporary, there is little doubt that the offices of preaching, pastoring, teaching, serving, and overseeing were intended to continue into the post-apostolic age. These distinctive forms of ministry are indispensable to the establishment, growth, and continuing needs of the Christian community. Wherever the church is found, these or similar offices of ministry will be found.

# The Premise of Apostolic Tradition Required But Variously Interpreted

The most common rite for mediating and continuing the intergenerational ministry in due succession from the apostles is ordination, the laying on of hands with prayer. Clement of Rome (A.D. 96) tells us that before their deaths the apostles appointed a successor apostolate to succeed them intergenerationally.

According to most pre-Reformation theories of historic succession, the apostles' authority passed to the bishops who succeeded them, and remains in those lines of bishops that converge backwards on the original bishops of the undivided church. This assumes an unbroken line of bishops to the present in an historic succession that is viewed as an element essential to Christianity. Diverse Protestant views tend to focus on the variable development of offices of ministry, deemphasizing priestly functions.

According to a broader, more flexible Protestant symbolic theory of confessional apostolic succession, the rock upon which the church is built is the confession of the apostles of Christ's lordship, and wherever that confession is duly made, there is apostolic succession.

It is unlikely that there will emerge a truly ecumenical sense of ministry without a unifying principle that embraces both of these sets of historical memories, and that allows the inquiry to take some ameliorative shape. I am seeking to formulate a doctrine of ministry grounded in the ancient consensual tradition that will be easily recognizable to both evangelicals and Catholics, both scholastics and charismatics, as consistent with their varied traditions of memory, all grounded in the most ancient layers of Christian tradition and experience.

Ordained Christian ministry is a gift of the Spirit by which the church administers the means of grace. Ministry is "not a new device appointed by men," but "a most ancient ordinance of God himself," who has always called ministers for the gathering, preservation, and guidance of his people (Second Helvetic Conf., CC, p. 150).

However variable the theories of succession, there is general agreement that there is continuity between the ministries and institutions of the old covenant and the new covenant. Christ willed to build upon the Apostle's confession a church where the Gospel would be preached and the means of grace administered according to his own initiative and ordering. The church's ministry functions so as to manifest and express the nature of the church. The forming of ministry is not merely to be regarded as a convenient arrangement, but rather an abiding structural feature of the body of Christ (Hall, DT, VIII, p. 53), a permanent feature that is constitutive of the organism, however variable in historic content.

# Interlude: A Request for a Hasty Wedding

I am going to suggest another case study for reflection, with the hope that these complex disciplinary issues can be brought closer to the arena of confessional practice.

Keith Naylor and Jane Nesbitt have requested an early date for their wedding in the church in which you serve as pastor. They want to be married very soon. There has been no time to ascertain impediments. One of the parties is unbaptized. There has been no interest shown in premarital counsel. Both the Naylor family and the Nesbitt family have served the church well and supported it heartily over many decades. The Naylors want to slow down the momentum of planning. The Nesbitts are putting pressure on you to set a date soon.

How would you devise a pastoral strategy for dealing with this disciplinary dilemma. State a sequence of actions you would take as an expression of the integrity of the eucharistic community and the apostolic tradition. Will you set a date for the wedding? If not, what then?

# Recapitulation

In Parts One and Two I have set forth a basic lay course in apostolic ministry, church discipline, and governance. While the language has often pointed toward the responsibilities of sacred or ordained ministry, I have emphasized throughout that the tasks of ordained ministry are derivative from the general ministry of the whole baptized people of God. Far from being an out-of-the-way subject for lay persons, it is crucial for laity to have a basic understanding of the priestly, prophetic, and governance roles of the whole apostolate.

Christ's prophetic, priestly, and governing ministries continue to work correctively within the body of Christ. Through the helping ministry (*diakonos*) Christ presents himself to the world as lowly servant. Through the ministry of teaching and guidance (*presbyteros*) Christ presents himself to the world as proclaimer of the truth. Through the ministry of oversight (*episkopos*) Christ presents himself to the world as head of the redeemed body. These orders of ministry have produced polity types that in some points of their history overstress one or the other of the offices, but taken in their complementarity, each has contributed providentially to the ecumenical whole. It is the whole people of God, the community of believers, the worshiping faithful, who share in Christ's prophetic, priestly and governance ministries, and not the orders of ordained ministry alone. This whole body of Christ, the people of God, are rightly understood to exercise a spiritual priesthood, since by faith they participate in Christ's priestly office each time they intercede for sinners. This whole body of Christ, the people of God, have a share in Christ's ministry of governance when they order their families and vocations and political lives under the revealed Word.

This whole people of God are represented in the service of worship in an orderly way by duly ordained ministers called of God and elected by due process into the ministry of Word and Sacrament. Grace is present in this setting aside of persons for representative ministry, for the essence of the service of ordination is the prayer for the grace that enables it. Neither in Israel nor in the apostolic church nor in the church today does the health of the laity flourish without sacred ministry. The authorization to sacred orders rests upon Jesus' own intention and specific directive.

Part Three

# Political Restraint in Eschatological Perspective

# 10

# The Value of Ecclesial Discipline to the *Polis*

How does discipline in the civil order differ from discipline within the redeemed, caring community of faith?

## Reordering the Relation of *Ekklēsia* and *Polis*

The *ekklēsia* is a community called of God, born of faith, enlivened by hope, joined by love. It exists primarily to treat illnesses of the human spirit. It does not use force to bring persons through its doors. Its only door is Spirit-engendered faith. One who believes and is baptized becomes confirmed by choice. There is no room for compulsion. That belongs to the state.

The forms of governance exercised by the church are primarily spiritual, although some temporal needs must be supplied. Buildings must be maintained, bills paid, letters written, as long as the church remains in history. But the kingdom sought by all these efforts is finally, as Jesus said, "not of this world" (John 18:36).

No political principle is more fundamental than the eschatological maxim that finally "each of us will give an account of himself to God" (Rom. 14:12). The pivotal eschatological principle that best secures a more just state is the premise that every individual must finally give account to God on the last day. This implies that every discrete political decision in the civil order (like every other moral decision) bears significantly upon the character of the believer or unbeliever with respect to their eternal destiny.

From this vital spiritual center, every corollary decision on the political circumference is affected. All trusts are exercised and all opportunities responded to in relation to this sense of ultimate accountability that finally will occur one by one before the righteous God. Every voter, police officer, judge, legislator, bureaucrat, recipient of welfare, and taxpayer must finally undergo this final investigative judgment.

# The Partisan Spirit

Political parties play a significant guiding and ordering role in democratic processes. It must not be regarded as offensive to Christian conscience to participate in a political party. But such participation is always prone to idolatrous distortions and opinionated divisiveness that runs counter to the universality of catholic love in the living church.

Since clergy serve persons of many parties and political ideologies, it is especially advisable that those who serve at the Lord's table not become inordinately identified with a single party or adversarial ideological commitment, lest the possibility of ministry of Word and Sacrament be constricted by unwarranted partisanship.

Christian political choice is an act of individual conscience. Each voter and legislator and executive office holder and judge is called finally to decide for himself or herself. For Christians, this decision is understood to occur *coram Deo*, as if veritably in God's presence. Christians make these choices prayerfully and seriously under the moral guidance of the teaching of the apostolate and the treasures of its sacred page. A political choice is an act of conscience that is free to associate with a political party, since the collective will normally works through the struggle of parties for the better interpretation of the proximate historical truth and justice of a particular political situation.

But that partisan choice must always come under the scrutiny of eschatological reasoning and moral self-examination. The Gospel calls the believer in the political order to embody compassion for those who differ. The partisan spirit, which is so contrary to apostolic love, has difficulty telling the truth in a way that seeks empathy with the neighbor in the other party.

Party loyalties that suppress conscience must be actively resisted. Political judgment rightly brings one to the bar of divine judgment. The Christian in the political order is called upon insofar as possible to "Test everything. Hold on to the good. Avoid every kind of evil" (1 Thess. 5:21–22).

It is not fitting to make instrumental political use of the confessing community, which is provided for preaching and Sacrament and authorized to engage in pastoral care. It is a distortion to use that community for overt, coarse, direct political purposes and partisan activities. Those to whom is committed the teaching office of the church have the duty of teaching according to Scripture concerning those commands, requirements, laws, maxims, duties, and mediating principles that impinge upon the conscience in political decision. Yet this must be done without unnecessary partisanship, leaving to each person the struggle of conscience before God.

# The State—Neither One, Nor Holy, Nor Catholic, Nor Apostolic

The church's functions and purposes are liturgical, evangelical, pedagogical, and sacramental. These differ markedly from the state's functions and the purposes of political order, the chief of which are civil tranquility, justice under law, and the protection of the commonweal.

The state is obviously neither apostolic by necessity or by definition, nor is it holy, catholic or one as is the church in its essential definition (Ursinus, Comm. on Heid. Catech., p. 291, cf. LS, Part 3). States are many, bound by civil laws for the maintenance of order and civic tranquility.

Since a particular state serves in a particular time and place, not all times and places, it cannot by definition be either one or catholic, for there is no universal state, only particular states. Since spatially, temporally, and territorially defined, the state cannot be catholic or universal or eternal. The state is limited by geographical space to a particular territory. The *communio sanctorum* is instead universal, having no political boundaries. The state makes no pretense to be or become holy or apostolic, though the state may accountably view its own identity or mission as accountable to the holy, and may be instructed or even edified by the teaching of the revealed Word.

No civil authority, however mighty, has the slightest legitimate power to administer Word and Sacrament. It does have legitimate authority and responsibility to secure civil tranquility for its citizens, whether or not they live by faith. "The chief duty of the civil magistrate is to procure and maintain peace and public tranquillity. . . Let him protect widows, fatherless children, and those that be afflicted, against wrong; let him repress, yea, and cut off, such as are unjust, whether in deceit or by violence" (Second Helvetic Conf., CC, p. 190).

The state has the power to take away the offender's freedom (by imprisoning) or, in some jurisdictions, even one's life (by capital punishment). The church has no power over the bodies of persons except in extreme cases to exclude its own communicants from joining the living Lord at his table. State power is physical and legal. Church power is moral and sacramental.

It was an established political order that unjustly declared of Jesus: "We have a law, and according to that law he must die, because he claimed to be the Son of God" (John 19:7).

# Not of This World:
# Distinguishing Word and Sword

The state governs by coercive means, using when necessary the power of the sword. Coercion is the distinctive power of the state, implying legitimate authority to enforce obedience with penalties under due process of just law. No church has that right or power or competence. The church has no coercive means and exercises only the persuasive means of the power of the word.

The Servant Messiah made it conspicuously clear that "my

kingdom is not of this world" (John 18:36). The coming reign of God's love is not of this world in the sense that it is sharply distinguishable from the coercion that is required for civil order. Meanwhile the church constantly meets and interfaces with the *saeculum* in humble service and accountability (Apostolic Constitutions, II.20.3, ANF VII, pp. 404-405; W. Temple, Church and Nation, I,II; D. Stone, pp. 40–51), rendering to Caesar what belongs to Caesar (Ambrose, Letters, 10ff., NPNF 2 X, pp. 422–30).

History judges harshly those who try gullibly and over-simply to combine Christianity and political interests. For when religious and secular interests too uncritically intertwine, each tends to be corrupted by the other. "The weapons we fight with are not the weapons of the world. On the contrary, they have divine power to demolish strong-holds" (2 Cor. 10:4).

The church does better by disavowing every aspect of coercive jurisdiction, leaving political prerogatives primarily to the state, and domestic jurisdiction primarily to the family to whom it has been assigned by God (Calvin, Inst. 4.10, 11). Every ancillary form of legitimate coercion is derived either from that assigned to the family or to the state (Hall, DT VIII, p. 108; J.N. Figgis, Churches in the Modern State).

These same constraints apply to the church's relation to political movements, unimagined and imagined revo-lutions, programmatic political reforms, and public policy proposals. The church cannot assume legitimate jurisdiction over them, but may stand in relation to them through individual participants as a community of conscience and attentive partner in dialogue. To questions of competing temporal claims, Jesus answered: "Who made me a judge or divider over you?" (Luke 12:14, KJV). Neither the church or its leadership is duly authorized to act directly or preemp-tively as judge or divider of public policy, but only indirectly as conscience of political justice. The *ekklēsia* knows that "justice by its very nature bears a certain likeness to folly" (Lactantius, DI, FC 49, p. 362).

The state has the sword which the church has no authority

to wield. The church has the Word preached and the Word embodied in Sacrament which the state, to be a just state, must respect and not intrude upon. Doctrinal and ecclesial matters are beyond the state's competence and jurisdiction. Christian political theory gradually learned to ground positive law in the consent of the people, so that the legitimacy of a sovereign power must be grounded in popular consent by those who have the power to choose and remove magistrates (Marsiglio of Padua, Defender of the Peace, I.12).

The renewed covenant community is not a nation but a celestial city that embraces all nations, all classes, both sexes. Any adult who repents with faith is eligible to be baptized, yet none could rightly be compelled to be baptized (Moss, CF, pp. 318–20).

The Roman Council of A.D. 863 warned that since spiritual and carnal efforts differ so radically, state power must not take to itself the rights of the *ekklēsia*, nor may the *ekklēsia* usurp the power of the state: "Since the same 'mediator of God and man, the man Christ Jesus' (1 Tim. 2:5) by His own acts and distinct dignities, has so decreed the duties of each power, *wishing His own to be lifted up by His salutary humility*, not to be submerged again by human pride. . . . Finally, we are completely without knowledge of how those to whom it has been intrusted only to be in charge of human affairs presume to judge concerning those through whom divine affairs are ministered" (Nicolas I, SCD 333, pp. 133–134, italics added). This is a humbling statement of the unique power of the meekness of faith in the presence of civil power. There was similar intent in the traditional formula that the magistracy is superior to sacred ministry in those things that pertain to the world, while the ministry is superior to magistracy in those things that pertain to God (Hugh of St. Victor, On the Sacraments, II.2.6, p. 257; cf. Robert Pullen, Sententiae, VII.7, MPL 186.625ff.).

# The *Ekklēsia* Has Civil Rights and Participates in the Civil Order

The church in a local community may be constituted as a legal entity and for purposes of temporal accountability has rights and duties under the law, but legal rights and civil status says nothing whatever about the church's status in the presence of God, or its distinctive mission or identity. Civil rights grow out of the ancillary fact that the church has social and historical placement in a particular society and legal system, by which it is considered a voluntary association, for that is what it looks like from a sociological-political point of view—even though this ignores the deeper fact that Christ is forming and extending his body in time. On this level of perception, the church has neither more nor less civil rights than other religious communities in a given society. Its members act wherever reasonably possible to insure freedom of speech and freedom of religion, without which the church is hard put to continue its mission.

Paul did not hesitate to appeal to due process of law as a right belonging to him as a Roman citizen (Acts 16:37; 22:25). Yet it is said that Ezra "was ashamed to ask the king for soldiers and horsemen to protect us from enemies on the road," for the "hand of our God is upon everyone who looks to him" (Ezra 8:22). The church similarly "should be ashamed to depend for revenue upon the state, although its members as citizens may justly demand that the state protect them in their rights of worship" (Strong, ST, p. 899).

At times the church must appeal to the state—"that rhinoceros" (Gregory I, Moralia, XXXI.5.7)—to protect her civil rights. But this protection is as costly as it is imperfect: "Will the wild ox consent to serve you? Will he stay by your manger at night? Can you hold him to the furrow with a harness?" (Job 39:9–10a). The church is powerless in the worldly sense in the presence of coercive power, which never yields to long term domestication. If harnessed in one generation it may break out in another.

The church has survived many hazardous political situations long before the modern world supposedly "came of age." Christians believe that the political welfare of the human community is never better served than by that which is the natural result of the teaching of the Gospel. The facts of history run counter to the "time-worn accusation that the Church is incompatible with the welfare of the commonwealth, and incapable of contributing to those things" (Leo XIII, Immortale Dei, COC II, p. 557).

The church, from the very nature of her being, looks to the celestial city and seeks the salvation of souls. Nonetheless she also "secures even in the mere order of perishable things advantages so many and so great that she could not do more even if she had been founded primarily and specially to secure prosperity in this life which is spent upon earth. In truth wherever the Church has set her foot she has at once changed the aspect of affairs, colored the manners of the people as with new virtues so also with a refinement unknown before" (Leo XIII, Immortale Dei, COC II, p. 555).

## The First Freedom: Religion

The apostolate claims as the most fundamental human right the freedom to preach the Gospel to every creature (Barth, Church and State; B. Haering, The Liberty of the Children of God). "The Church should enjoy that full measure of freedom which her care for the salvation of men requires. This is a sacred freedom, because the only-begotten Son endowed it with the Church which He purchased with His blood" (Vat. II, Free 13).

"God alone is Lord of the conscience, and he has left it free from the doctrines and commandments of men which are contrary to his word or not contained in it. Church and state should be separate. The state owes to the church protection and full freedom in the pursuit of its spiritual ends. In providing for such freedom no ecclesiastical group or denomination should be favored by the state more than others" (Southern Baptist Convention, 1925, CC, p. 350).

The most profound way the church affects state policy and power is one by one—by converting those who vote or exercise legitimate power, by offering new spiritual life to those placed in vocations in the world, who are thereby able to touch the world with God's grace and truth. The serving church follows the steps of the serving Lord in going about quietly doing good, in constantly looking for ways to allow faith to become active in love, to engage in good works for the succor of the needy, employing whatever institutional means are reasonably available to implement these works of mercy that refract God's own mercy.

Yet these works are an expression of faith, not its essence, not the primary purpose for which the church is called into being, which is to proclaim the good news of God's coming and freely to offer the duly instituted means of grace. When good works become a substitute for faith's response to grace, then they have no saving efficacy and may come to be an obstacle to the service of the neighbor.

Since the Constantinian period, the church has from time to time been drawn into cozy relationships with better and worse national entities, so as to become an established religion of an entire realm or nation, a national or established church, as in Kierkegaard's Danish "Christendom," Czarist Russia, Franco Spain, or Elizabethan England. Accordingly, everyone born into that realm is routinely baptized *pro forma*. Are such churches true churches? Is such baptism valid baptism? Scripture attests that the church exists only where it is freely chosen, where grace awakens free responsiveness. Church establishments have deflated and defaced the currency of Christian baptism, regeneration, and *koinonia*. Yet we cannot assume that the divine economy intends to work always and only apart from established church-state relationships. For we have seen powerful evidences of the Spirit's work within them. Jesus himself spoke of tares among the wheat, and the dragnet cast into the sea which gathers all kinds of fish.

# Interlude: A Case of Changed
# Sexual Orientation

A general assembly of a denomination has repeatedly held officially that homosexuality is incompatible with Christian teaching, and that self-avowed practicing homosexuals cannot be admitted into the sacred ministries in which sustained intimate confidential relations are expected between minister and parishioner. George is a minister who as a married heterosexual was ordained. Later he became a self-avowed practicing homosexual. Should his ordination be continued? Should legal defense money be given by church agencies to defend him legally?

# Recapitulation

The corrective task of admonition which occurs primarily within the tranquil precincts of the disciplined community has urgent relevance for the environing world. Ecclesial discipline in its own quiet way has decisive value for the saeculum. The safety, justice, and tranquillity of the world is enhanced by permitting the church simply to be itself, to proclaim its word and exercise its communion discipline.

Discipline in the civil order, with its legitimated capacity to exercise coercion, differs radically from discipline within the redeemed, caring community of faith. The state is not well served by commandeering the church on behalf of partisan political objectives. However indispensable within the conditions of the history of sin, the state is neither one, nor holy, nor catholic, nor apostolic. The state can only live by the sword, while the faithful are being freed to live by the Word. Though ordered by a principle different from that of the state, the church has civil rights and participates responsibly in civil order. What the state owes primarily to the church is the freedom within the church to proclaim and order itself under the Gospel.

# 11

# Corrective Love as an Implicit Political Theology

By what means is the reconciling community sustained amid its hazardous transit through political change? How is the relation between the worshiping community and the political process to be reunderstood and reshaped amid the collapse of modernity?

## The Disciplinary Role of Civil Magistracy

The political task of the church is not to politicize the *ekklēsia* in the world's terms, but to sanctify the *ekklēsia* on its own terms as a deciding community. By embodying its mission to the world, it will, one by one, effect constructive change in the larger society.

The state restrains the violence toward which sinners are prone. The state provides a context of law in which the ordering of human relationships of accountability is possible.

However abused as an instrument of justice, the need for law and order (and hence for the state) remains constant amid the history of sin. Hence a proximate awe for civil magistracy is a work of preparing and ordering grace (John Chrysostom, Hom. on the Statues, NPNF 1 IX, pp. 381–83). Some public order is necessary to prevent the flood of human self-assertiveness from overflowing its bounds with self-destructive fury.

That the state is a grace-enabled and providentially-administered order, not merely an artifact of human contrivance, is abundantly clear from Scripture (Rom. 13:1–4; 1 Pet. 2:13–14), though all its gifts and possibilities are distortable. There is no political achievement that is incorruptible, and no form of political imagination that can finally relax its guard against sin, and no political scheme that can guarantee its values in perpetuity.

Paul bluntly appealed to Christians even under the dubious conditions of Roman rule: "Everyone must submit himself to the governing authorities, for there is no authority except that which God has established. The authorities that exist have been established by God. Consequently, he who rebels against the authority is rebelling against what God has instituted, and those who do so will bring judgment on themselves. For rulers hold no terror for those who do right, but for those who do wrong" (Rom. 13:1–3).

"Lawful civil ordinances are good works of God," argued the Augsburg Confession, wherein believers have a right to "bear civil office, to sit as judges . . . to make legal contracts, to hold property," and "to be given in marriage" (Art. XVI, Neve, Luth. Sym., p. 249). Insofar as civil authority resists evil and seeks justice, and helps all live in peace and tranquillity, it is to be obeyed (1 Tim. 2:2).

# The Creative Tension Between Obedience to God and to the State

Though Christians maintain allegiance to a heavenly city that transcends all earthly forms of governance (Phil. 3:20), this does not justify or invite indifference to or neglect of civil accountability amid the earthly city. The divine economy calls for the use and transformation of historical and human institutions and powers toward the increase of justice and love of God and humanity.

The tension between Roman 13:1 and Acts 5:29 is expressed in the Augsburg Confession: "Christians are obliged to be subject to civil authority and obey its commands and laws in all that can be done without sin. But when commands of the civil authority cannot be obeyed without sin, we must obey God rather than men" (Acts 5:29; Art. XVI, CC, p. 73; cf. Calvin, Inst. 4.20.22–29). If legitimate civil authority derives ultimately from God, illegitimate civil authority must be called to question as a distortion of the divine claim.

The New Hampshire Confession wisely advised "that civil government is of divine appointment, for the interests and good order of human society; and that magistrates are to be prayed for, conscientiously honored, and obeyed, except in things opposed to the will of our Lord Jesus Christ, who is the only Lord of the conscience, and the Prince of the kings of the earth" (CC, p. 339). "Infidelity or difference in religion doth not make void the magistrate's just and legal authority, nor free the people from their due obedience to him: from which ecclesiastical persons are not exempted" (Westminster Conf., XXIII.4, CC, p. 220; cf. Thirty-nine Articles, XXXVII, CC, p. 279). "The Church ought to pray for the government that it may walk in righteousness. The Church should also let its voice be heard by the government" (Batak Confession, XII, CC, pp. 563–64).

# The Mission of Corrective Love amid the Violence of the World

The church like her Lord has no place finally to lay her head. She makes her witness to the eternal God within the conditions of human history, not in a fantasized non-spatial, non-temporal world. The church has just as much right as other institutions in the civil order to own property legally, to maintain a place of worship, to collect and distribute charities according to good accounting procedures and by fair methods and with open accounts, and where necessary to use legal counsel to help guarantee its civil rights.

The Gospel announces and enables "peace, good will toward men" (Luke 2:14, KJV), but it also requires lawful resistance to those who harm others. War brings evidence of the enormity of human sin in collective forms, but given the monstrous history of sin, it is at times necessary to resist coercive forms of injustice when all other diplomatic and non-coercive means have been exhausted. A nation lacking a police force or capacity for military defense risks unjustly making its citizens vulnerable to the aggressions that inevitably accompany sin. Though "such things" as war and violence and famine "must happen," nonetheless "see to it that you are not alarmed," for "the end is still to come" (Matt. 24:6). All unjust human violence will finally have to become accountable to the Just One at the end of history. Hence the spectacle of unjust human violence is viewed in Scripture as analogous to "birth pains" (Matt. 24:8).

Christian political thought has affirmed that Christians may "engage in just wars and serve as soldiers" (Augsburg Conf., XX). As horrible as war is, it is not as horrible as allowing free reign to those who would reek unmitigated violence upon the innocent. Christian conscience puts moral constraints upon the uses of the weapons of war, especially as the cost-benefit calculus of defensive war becomes diminished by huge casualties of innocent non-combatants.

Often the nations do not understand their role in providential history, so wrapped up are they in the egocentric assertion of national interest (cf. Dan. 2:31–45). Nations, like individuals, are born, grow, flourish, fade, and die. Each nation in each time is given special challenges and callings and responsibility distinctive of that time, and every citizen in that nation will be called to final accountability to God for decisions made individually and collectively.

The Barmen Declaration repudiated the false teaching that "there are areas of our life in which we belong not to Jesus Christ but another lord, areas in which we do not need justification and sanctification through him. . . that the state can and should expand beyond its special responsibility to become the single and total order of human life" (CC, p. 521).

When citizens are no longer deemed responsible for caring for themselves, or for productivity in a free market, but are paternalistically cared for by the state under the direction of knowledge-elites, then human self-initiative and freedom are undermined. When command economies play the game of "We pretend to work and they pretend to pay us," they put their societies on a long-term trajectory of demoralization, injustice, and increasing poverty.

## Whether Accommodation of the Church to the State Tends to Enrich or Debase the Currency of Christian Discipline

The church is called to serve the world, become a means of blessing to the world, become regenerative leaven within and for each temporal society and institution. But it is not thereby being called to become a competitor with the state, or a substitute state, or an ersatz arm of political action. It is fitting that the church not attempt to exercise control or authority within the state, and that the state acknowledge, without tending toward religious establishment, the transcendent claim of final judgment as significant for its present decisions (Luther, LW 45:91ff.).

Church and state have overlapping interests in crucial arenas such as education, marriage, and issues of social justice. The complete exclusion of the church from the realm of decision making in the state is neither possible or desirable (Calvin, Inst., 4.20; Schultz, CD&ST, pp. 187–89).

State power is best limited and constrained by moral discernment grounded in religious awareness. The government which governs best is that which is required to coerce least, wherein the conscience of the people is already well instructed by good and reasonable moral teaching.

The legislative processes of particular church bodies normally provide for a fit ordering of public worship and governance of church temporal affairs. They do well "not to intermeddle with civil affairs which concern the commonwealth, unless by way of humble petition in cases extraordinary; or by way of advice for satisfaction of conscience" (Westminster Conf., XXXI.3–5, CC, p. 228).

An oath asks God to witness what we are saying in our hearts, so that we will deceive neither ourselves nor others in formally or publicly undertaking a major responsibility, as in a court of law or in a pledge to defend civil justice. An oath to a legitimated civil authority is lawful when one's vocation in society requires that such a pledge be made or when the neighbor's welfare is imperiled or when every other form of hallowed commitment is exhausted (Chemnitz, Loci, I, 47ff.). It is evident from Scripture that righteous persons may commit themselves publicly in such oaths as a solemn act consistent with religious faith (Gen. 21:24; 31:53; Deut. 10:20; cf. Is. 45:23–24). Idolatrous, impulsive, or imprudent oaths are forbidden.

The alleged "communalism" of the Book of Acts was not a matter of coercive state policy, but an entirely voluntary matter undertaken to care for the family of faith. Nor was it a permanent or normative arrangement, otherwise communism would have become the prevailing economic system of ecumenical Christianity.

With the increasing influence of the Christian Gospel in society, some have expected the church to mature and vanish into the mechanisms of the state, which would gradually take over the functions heretofore undertaken by the church and the family. It is folly to imagine that the church will gradually diminish as more and more of its functions are undertaken by civil government. For we live in a time when almost everything that civil government has undertaken has tended  toward spendthrift failure and moral catastrophe.

# The Usurpation of Legitimate Power by Church or State

There are two forms of usurpation of legitimate power in the church-state relation, of *polis* by *ekklēsia*; and of *ekklēsia* by the *polis*.

The power legitimately granted to the church is the power to proclaim the Word and celebrate the Sacraments and engage in pastoral care and disciplinary formation—all non-coercive functions. The church abuses this power when it seeks to wield the sword or inordinately influence the structures and administration of power, or limits the legitimate powers of the state, or puts pressure other than moral influence upon the legislative, judicial, or executive processes (Augsburg Conf., XXVIII). The disciplinary power of the keys "does not interfere at all with government or temporal authority" which is "concerned with matters altogether different from the Gospel" (Augsburg Conf., CC, p. 99).

The opposite form of usurpation of authority is that by the state over the church. When a civil magistrate seeks to regulate spiritual matters or conscience or preaching or Sacrament or worship or ordination, an intrusion occurs into the legitimate power that belongs to religious communities and deserves the protection of civil authorities.

## Social Accountability amid the History of Sin

Paul urged all individuals to seek to be radically accountable in whatever historical situation they find themselves, whether relatively just or unjust. Since "you were bought at a price" on the cross, "do not become slaves of men" (1 Cor. 7:23). Those who died with Christ to the world are asked "why, as though you still belonged to it, do you submit to its rules: 'Do not handle! Do not taste! Do not touch'?"—rules which have only "an appearance of wisdom" (Col. 2:20–23).

"We have to make of the Church in every place a voice for those who have no voice, and a home where every man will be at home. . . to every system, every programme and every person that treats any man as though he were an irresponsible thing" (Amsterdam Assembly, WCC, CC, p. 576).

Meanwhile those who find themselves bound under oppressive conditions are instructed to become accountable within historical structures of proximate justice, even if these political structures remain conspicuously unjust, and to continue to respond to oppressors "with respect" and "with sincerity of heart, just as you would obey Christ," not to win the favor of man but "doing the will of God from your heart. Serve wholeheartedly, as if you were serving the Lord, not men" (Eph. 6:5–7).

The political health of the *polis* is better served by this radical, eschatological understanding of accountability than by a grudging, class-conscious grasping, or pretentious revolutionary mentality, pretentious because it pretends to be just while it is creating new structures of injustice.

In a democratic society everyone who has the franchise to vote must bear some responsibility for the diffuse injustices of the society. Social injustices are often very slow in being corrected, hence patience is a primary political virtue and rashness of imagination and judgment a leading political vice.

## Interlude: A Case of Civil Disobedience

You as a Christian mother are under strong moral conviction that abortion is the murder of children. A court order has prevented your group from picketing the abortion clinic. You are determined to make a protest. You find, however, that you likely will be arrested if you proceed. Your pastor advises you, on the basis of Romans 13, to obey the powers that be. You have decided to disobey your pastor and continue with the civil disobedience action. You are arrested and spend two nights in jail. On the second day your pastor visits you in jail. He still thinks you acted wrongly. And he is your spiritual advisor and pastor. What do you say to him?

## Recapitulation

The worshiping community is sustained by the Spirit amid its hazardous transit through political change. Though Christians maintain allegiance to a heavenly city that transcends all earthly forms of coercive governance, this does not justify or invite indifference to or neglect of civil accountability amid the earthly city. The Christian life does not as a matter of course pit accountability to the state against accountability to God. All unrighteousness finally becomes accountable to the Just One at the end of history.

Excessive accommodation of the church to the political order may debase the currency of Christian testimony. Just as the state has no right to usurp power in the arena of religious belief and conscience, so the church has no right to usurp power in the legislative, judicial or executive arenas of political authority. The church stands in the midst of the history of sin looking toward the final consummation of history in the promised return of her Lord.

# Conclusion

# Confession 101— A Summary

The thread of argument has taken these turns:

1. Corrective discipline is intrinsic to the well-being of God's household. The metaphor of the keys to God's dwelling place is central to Jesus' teaching of communion discipline. The keys refer to the pardon of God who welcomes contrite sinners into the coming reign of God. Christianity proclaims the power of God to free sinners from sin. If this good news is rejected, the rejector is left in self-chosen bondage of the will.

The gates of hell shall never finally prevail against the onslaught this victorious Word of grace. Within history, this side of its consummation, human freedom remains tempted to despairing bondage to creaturely idolatries.

2. The most gentle of all nurturing tasks is tender, loving admonition. The work of gentle correction is closely related to the epitome of Christian community: the eucharistic Sacrament of reconciliation. By the grace of baptism, the believer is offered a newly regenerated life empowered by the Spirit. When sin occurs after baptism it is fitting prior to coming to the eucharistic table to ask forgiveness for sins, with sincere intent toward reparation and fundamental behavioral change.

By its prayer for pardon the church conveys the forgiving Word to the penitent. Absolution completes confession of sin and joins it with confession of Christ. Three forms of absolution are found with varying energies in different periods of Christian history: petitionary absolution which earnestly prays that the penitent will be forgiven; kerygmatic absolution, in which the church proclaims that the forgiveness of sins is a fact because of the redeeming work of Christ; and personally authoritative absolution which makes a concrete statement that this particular penitent is forgiven of sins, by saying "I absolve you," with specificity.

The regular opportunity for private confession to God has been lost sight of in the church that has tragically accommodated itself to the narcissistic and naturalistic assumptions of modernity. Postmodern faith is being freed to relearn and renew the ancient penitential practice of confession prior to eucharistic celebration.

3. The way is narrow that leads to life. There is no justification without faith, and no faith without godly repentance, which calls for a complete change of mind, heart, and will in turning away from the power of sin to receive the forgiving Word.

In administering the Sacrament of reconciliation, sins which are prone to lead to spiritual death are more crucially the concern of gentle admonition than those lighter sins which do not inevitably tend toward spiritual death. Care-givers in the body of Christ must be attentive to the difference.

There are in classic Christianity three gateways of forgiveness: baptism, prayer, and reconciliation after public penitence. The grace of repentance is offered in response to the veritable call of the living Lord and is not to be treated reductionistically as if merely a social artifact. In the apostolic tradition the Spirit has provided a means of intergenerational transmission of disciplinary authority to the reconciling community. The task of loving discipline is renewed in each generation of Christian experience by reappropriating the apostolic tradition.

4. The community of faith has no coercive power, only the persuasive power to invite believers to the feast of divine forgiveness, and in grave cases to ask penitents not to appear at the Lord's table until fitting acts of repentance and reparation are done. While every communicant has the civil

right to withdraw from the community of faith and thus to avoid that corrective judgment which belongs within the circle of faith, the eucharistic community may for the good of the community or the individual withhold the eucharist from the obdurate in hopes of repentance and reconciliation.

The reconciling Sacrament is not intended for the recalcitrant impenitent, but the repenting faithful. The disciplinary exclusion of the impenitent from the Lord's table has a restorative intent. The incorrigible bring judgment upon themselves by their impenitence.

5. In opinions not necessary for salvation, much room is left for prudential judgment in the ministry of confession. The confessor keeps steadily to the course of asking how conscience is directing the conversation. The pastor who does not have time to listen to human hurt is hardly fit for the ministry of pardon. There are times when it is better to say nothing than something.

6. It is the Holy Spirit who forms, orders, and configures the confessing community, its preaching, praise, prayer, sacramental life, and mission. Administry is that form of ministry that makes way for other forms of ministry. The engendering Administrator of salvation is God the Holy Spirit. There is no single form of disciplinary administry that applies to all historical situations, but rather an ever-emergent requirement to look for proximately just and useful forms of disciplinary governance in the light of specific historic limitations.

Whoever with Spirit-born faith voluntarily accepts membership in the body of Christ thereby decides to be subject to its structures of discipline, admonition, and governance. The primitive church was flexible in its search for consultative and proto-democratic modes of decision-making insofar as they were consonant with the apostolic witness. Various liturgical traditions understandably have grown up expressing salutary varieties and cultural-historical differences within the one, holy, catholic, apostolic church.

7. Complementary lay and clerical spheres of accountability always interface in the administration of discipline. Neither laity nor clergy are unilaterally or exclusively responsible for gyroscopic course corrections in the trajectory of the one, holy, catholic, apostolic church through history. Rather the *laos* is a single whole people of God. It is for their sake that the *klēros* are assigned distinctive guardianship tasks.

The default of corrective discipline by hyperliberated clergy does not finally exempt the laity from accountability, since the whole *laos* remains responsible for attending to its own health. Since the church's mission is not simply the mission of the clergy, the whole *laos* must take responsibility for the negligence of ordained ministers in guarding the apostolic tradition of discipline. It is only through the lay apostolate working through many vocations that the leaven of the Gospel penetrates the world. No doctrine has become orthodox simply by clerical definition, but only by consent to apostolic teaching.

8. The apostolic tradition of admonition awaits retrieval amid postmodern culture. Intrinsic to the work of corrective love is the development of an ordered apostolic ministry. The mission of the apostolate is defined by the Lord himself in his Great Commission: to proclaim the Gospel to the world, to teach, to make disciples, and to baptize in the triune name. The time of the apostolate is the entire history between Pentecost and Parousia. Only by adaptably responding to changing historical challenges is the mission of the one, holy, catholic apostolate actualized.

Disciplinary administry was founded by Jesus himself in his training of the Twelve for proclamation, teaching, discipling, and the ordering of time through worship. It was from the synagogue that the early Christian *ekklēsia* derived its basic models of discipline and governance. The synagogue eldership was reshaped into the church's office of *presbyter*.

All who share in the body of Christ implicitly are by their confirmation of their baptism giving assent to apostolic teaching, and placing themselves under the discipline of an ordered ministry. Although the offices of ministry went through complex historical development, that development is organically grounded in the personal relation between Jesus and his disciples. By the end of the primitive apostolic age, the orders of ministry were sufficiently defined to be able to develop in a versatile way so as to relate to new historical challenges without losing their primary identity as the embodiment of Christ's own minister.

9. Christ's prophetic, priestly, and governing ministries continue to work correctively within the continuing body of Christ. Through the helping ministry (*diakonos*) Christ presents himself to the hurting, guilt-laden, disordered world as lowly servant. Through the ministry of teaching and guidance (*presbyteros*) Christ presents himself to the world as proclaimer of the forgiving Word. Through the ministry of oversight (*episkopos*) Christ presents himself to the world as shepherd-king and head of the reconciling community. These orders of ministry have produced polity types that in some points of their history have overly accentuated one or the other of the offices, but taken in their complementarity, each is needed to sustain the oneness, holiness, catholicity and apostolicity of the church.

It is the whole people of God, the community of believers, the worshiping faithful, who share in Christ's prophetic, priestly and governance ministries, and not the ordained ministry alone. This whole body of Christ, the people of God, exercise a spiritual priesthood in which by faith they participate in Christ's priestly office each time they intercede for sinners. This whole body of Christ, the people of God, are rightly understood to have a share in Christ's ministry of governance when they order their families and vocations and political lives under the revealed Word.

This whole people of God are represented in the service of worship in an orderly way by duly ordained ministers called of God and elected by due process into the ministry of Word and Sacrament. Grace is present in this setting aside of persons for representative ministry, for the essence of ordination is the prayer for the grace that enables it. Neither in Israel nor the apostolic church nor the church today does the health of the laity flourish without sacred ministry. The authorization to sacred orders rests upon Jesus' own intention and specific directive.

10. The corrective task of admonition which occurs primarily within the more tranquil precincts of the disciplined community has relevance for the environing world. Ecclesial discipline in its own quiet way has decisive meaning for the *saeculum*. The safety, justice, and tranquillity of the world is enhanced when the church is permitted simply to be itself, to exercise its communion discipline.

Discipline within the redeemed, caring community of faith differs radically from magistracy in the civil order, with its legitimated capacity to exercise coercion under law. The state is not well served by commandeering the church on behalf of partisan political objectives. However indispensable within the conditions of the history of sin, the state is neither one, nor holy, nor catholic, nor apostolic. The state can only live by the sword, while the faithful are being freed to live by the Word. Though ordered by a principle different from that of the state, the church has civil rights and participates in civil responsibilities. What the state owes to the church is the freedom to proclaim and order itself under the Gospel.

11. The worshiping community is sustained by the Spirit amid its hazardous transit through political change. Though Christians maintain allegiance to a heavenly city that transcends all earthly forms of governance, this does not justify indifference to or neglect of civil accountability amid the earthly city. The Christian life does not as a matter of course pit accountability to the state against accountability to God. All unrighteousness finally becomes accountable to the

Just One at the end of history.

Excessive accommodation of the church to the political order may debase the currency of Christian testimony. Just as the state has no right to usurp power in the arena of religious belief and conscience, so the church has no right to usurp power in the legislative, judicial, or executive arenas of political authority. The church stands in the midst of the history of sin looking toward the final consummation of history in the promised return of her Lord.

---

"O Lord, we beseech Thee, mercifully hear our prayers, and spare all those who confess their sins unto Thee; that they, whose consciences by sin are accused, by Thy merciful pardon may be absolved, through Jesus Christ our Lord"
(Commination Service to be used on Ash Wednesday,
Book of Common Prayer).

# Abbreviations

| | |
|---|---|
| ACW | Ancient Christian Writers: The Works of the Fathers in Translation. Edited by J. Quasten, J.C. Plumpe, and W. Burghardt. 44 vols. New York: Paulist Press, 1946– |
| AF | The Apostolic Fathers. Edited by J. N. Sparks. New York: Thomas Nelson, 1978 |
| Ag. | Against |
| AEG | Ante-Nicene Exegesis of the Gospels. 6 vols. Edited by Harold D. Smith. London: S.P.C.K., 1925 |
| ANF | Ante-Nicene Fathers. Edited by A. Roberts and J. Donaldson. 10 vols. 1885–1896. Reprinted ed., Grand Rapids, MI: Eerdmans, 1979. Book (in Roman numerals) and chapter or section number (usually in Arabic numberals), followed by volume and page number. |
| APT | Tertullian, Apologetic and Practical Treatises, ed. C. Dodgson. Oxford: J.H. Parker, 1854. |
| BCP | Book of Common Prayer (1662). Royal Breviar's edition. London: S.P.C.K., n.d. |
| BEM | Baptism, Eucharist, and Ministry. Geneva: World Council of Churches, 1982 |
| Bk. | Book |
| BOC | The Book of Concord, (1580). Edited by T. G. Tappert. Philadelphia: Muhlenberg Press, 1959. |
| BPR | Book of Pastoral Rule. Gregory the Great. NPNF 2 XII |
| Catech. | Catechism or Catechetical |
| CC | Creeds of the Churches. Edited by John Leith. Richmond, VA: John Knox Press, 1979. |
| CCC | Creeds, Councils and Controversies, ed. J. Stevenson. London: SPCK, 1966. |
| CD | Church Dogmatics. Karl Barth. Edited by G. W. Bromiley, T. F. Torrance, et al. 4 vols. Edinburgh: T. & T. Clark, 1936-1969 |
| CD & ST | Christian Doctrine and Summary of Theology. Schultz, ed. Philadelphia: Lutheran Board of |

| | |
|---|---|
| | Publications, 1906 |
| CFS | Cistercian Fathers Series. 44 vols. to date. Kalamazoo, MI: Cistercian Publications, 1968– |
| CH | Church History. Eusebius of Caesarea. NPNF 2 I. |
| Ch | Dogmatic Constitution on the Church (Lumen Gentium), Doc. Vat. II |
| CHC | Ursinus. Commentary on Heidelberg Catechism |
| Chr. | Christian |
| C & A | Confession and Absolution. M. Dudley and G. Rowell, ed., London: SPCK, 1903 |
| C & Ab | Confession and Absolution. J. C. Winslow, London, 1960 |
| C&M | The Church and the Ministry. Charles Gore. London: Longmans, Green, 1910, 4th ed. |
| CMM | The Catechism of Modern Man: All in the Words of Vatican II, Boston: St. Paul Editions, 1967 |
| CMR | The Church, Ministry, and Reunion. W. Norman Pittenger. Greenwich: Seabury, 1957 |
| COC | Creeds of Christendom. Edited by P. Schaff. 3 vols. New York: Harper and Bros., 1919 |
| Comm. | 1. Commentary. 2. Commonitory. Vincent of Lerins, NPNF 2 XI |
| Compend. | Compendium of Christian Theology. William Burt Pope. 3 vols. New York: Phillips and Hunt, n.d. |
| Conf. | Confessions |
| CT | Christian Theology. Emery H. Bancroft. Edited by Ronald B. Majors. Grand Rapids: Zondervan, 1976 |
| CWI | Charles Journet, The Church of the Word Incarnate, London: Sheed and Ward, 1954, Volume I unless otherwise noted |
| CWS | Classics of Western Spirituality. Edited by Richard J. Payne et al. 30 vols. to date. Mahwah, NJ: Paulist Press, 12978-. |
| DI | Lactantius, Divine Institutes, FC 49 |
| DGF | To Declare God's Forgiveness. Clark Hyde, |

|  | Wilton, Conn; Morehouse-Barlow, 1984 |
| Doc. Vat. II | W.M. Abbott, ed. Documents of Vatican II. NY: America Press, 1966 |
| DT | Dogmatic Theology. Francis Hall. New York: Longmans, Green, and Co., 1907-1922 |
| DUCC | Dictionnaire universel et complete des Conciles, ed. Migne, Paris: Aux Ateliers Catholiques du Petit-Montrouge, 1847 |
| EA | D. Martin Luthers sämmtliche Werke, Frankfurt and Erlangen, 1826-57, Erlanger Ausgabe, volume number followed by page number |
| East. Orth. Catech. | Eastern Orthodox Catechism. Translated by F. S. Noli. Boston: Albaninan Orthodox Church of America, 1954 |
| EC | Essential Christianity. H. P. Hughes. London: Isbister and Co., 1894 |
| ECF | Early Christian Fathers. H. Bettenson, ed. Oxford: OUP, 1962 |
| ECW | Early Christian Writers: The Apostolic Fathers. Translated by Maxwell Staniforth. London: Penguin Books, 1968 |
| Evang. | Evangelical |
| EVO | Darwell Stone, Episcopacy and Valid Orders, New York: Longmans, Green and Co. 1900 |
| Fast | Paul VI, Apostolic Constitution on Fast and Abstinence, 1966 |
| FC | The Fathers of the Church: A New Translation. Edited by R. J. Deferrari. 69 vols. to date. Washington, DC: Catholic University Press, 1947– |
| Gk. | Greek |
| HCS | J. T. McNeill, A History of the Cure of Souls, New York: Harper & Bros., 1951 |
| Heid. | Heidelberg |
| Her. | Heresies |
| Hom. | Homily |
| IBC | Interpretation: A Bible Commentary for |

|  |  |
|---|---|
|  | Teaching and Preaching, Louisville: John Knox Press, Louisville, 1987– |
| Inst. | Institutes of the Christian Religion. John Calvin. LCC, vols. 20, 21. References by book and chapter number, at times followed by section number |
| JTS | Journal of Theological Studies |
| KJV | King James Version, Bible, 1611 |
| Lai | Decree on the Apostolate of the Laity (Apostolicam actuositatem), Doc. Vat. II |
| LCF | H. Bettenson, ed. Later Christian Fathers |
| LCC | The Library of Christian Classics. Edited by J. Baillie, J.T. McNeill, and H. P. Van Dusen. 26 vols. Philadelphia: Westminster, 1953–1961 |
| LEP | Of the Laws of Ecclesiastical Polity. 2 vols. Richard Hooker. New York: E.P. Dutton, 1960–3 |
| Loci | Melanchthon, Loci Commumnes Theologici, LCC XIX, pp. 18–154 |
| LS | Life in the Spirit. Thomas C. Oden. San Francisco: Harper Collins, 1991 |
| LT | Loci Theologici (1610-21). 22 vols. John Gerhard. Tübingen: n.p., 1762–87 |
| Luth. Sym. | Introduction to Lutheran Symbolics. J .L. Neve. Burlington, Iowa: German Literary Board, 1917 |
| L W | Luther's Works. American Edition, eds. Jaroslav Pelikan and Helmuth T. Lehmann, 56 vols. St. Louis: Concordia Publishing House and Philadelphia: Fortress Press, 1956ff. |
| Mand. | Mandates, Pastor of Hermas, ANF II |
| MLS | Martin Luther: Selections From His Writings. John Dillenberger, editor. NY: Doubleday, 1961 |
| MPG | Patrologia Graeca. Edited by J. B. Migne. 162 vols. Paris: Migne, 1857-1876. Volume number followed by column number |
| MPL | Patrologia Latina. Edited by J. B. Migne. 221 vols. Paris: Migne, 1841–1865. Volume number followed by column number. General Index, Paris, 1912 |

| | |
|---|---|
| MS | A. J. Gordon, The Ministry of the Spirit, Phila: American Baptist Publication Society, 1894 |
| MWS | Ministry, Word, and Sacrament. Martin Chemnitz. St. Louis: Concordia, 1981 |
| NDM | Nature and Destiny of Man. Reinhold Niebuhr. 2 vols. New York: Scribner's, 1941, 1943. |
| NEB | New English Bible |
| NIV | New International Version |
| NPNF | A Select Library of the Nicene and Post-Nicene Fathers of the Christian Church. 1st Series, 14 vols. 2nd series, 14 vols. Edited by H. Wace and P. Schaff. References by title and book or chapter, and subsection, and NPNF series no., volume and page number. New York: Christian, 1887-1900 |
| NRSV | New Revised Standard Version |
| OOT | Outlines of Theology. Archibald Alexander Hodge. Grand Rapids: Eerdmans, 1928 |
| Patr. | Patrology. J. Quasten. 3 vol. Westminster, MD: Christian Classics Inc., 1983-84 |
| PS | Personal Salvation. Wilbur Tillett. Nashville: Barbee and Smith, 1902 |
| SCD | Sources of Christian Dogma (Enchiridion Symbolorum). Edited by Henry Denzinger. Translated by Roy Deferrari. New York: Herder, 1954 |
| SCDoc. | System of Christian Doctrine. Isaak A. Dorner. Volume IV if not otherwise indicated. Edinburgh: T&T Clark, 1898 |
| SCF | 1 A Summary of the Christian Faith. Henry E. Jacobs. Philadelphia: General Council of Publications, 1905  2 SCF On the Sacraments of the Christian Faith. Hugh of St. Victor. Cambridge, MA: Mediaeval Academy of America, 1951 |
| Sim. | Similitudes, Pastor of Hermas. ANF II |
| ST | 1 J. Strong, Systematic Theology. 2 Summa Theologica. Thomas Aquinas. Edited by English Dominican Fathers. 3 vols. New York: Benziger, |

|         | 1947. References include part, sub-part, question number, volume and page number of Benziger edition. See STae for the Blackfriars edition. 3. T. Oden, Systematic Theology. 3 vols. San Francisco: Harper Collins, 1987–91 |
|---------|---|
| TC      | Training in Christianity. Soren Kierkegaard. Princeton: Princeton University Press, 1941 |
| TCI     | Amos Binney, Theological Compend Improved, with Daniel Steele. New York: Phillips and Hunt, 1875 |
| TDNT    | Theological Dictionary of the New Testament. Edited by G. Kittel. Translated by G. W. Bromiley. 9 vols. Grand Rapids, MI: Eerdmans, 1964–1974 |
| Tho. Aq. | Thomas Aquinas |
| TI      | Theological Institutes. Richard Watson. 2 vols. Edited by John M'Clintock. New York: Carlton & Porter, 1850 |
| Trent   | The Canons and Decrees of the Council of Trent, Ed. H. J. Schroeder, Rockford, IL: TAN, 1978 |
| Trin.   | Trinity |
| Vis.    | Visions, Pastor of Hermas. ANF II |
| WA      | Weimar Ausgabe. Werke, Martin Luther. Volume number followed by page number |
| WJW     | Works of the Rev. John Wesley. Edited by Thomas Jackson. 14 vols. London: Wesleyan Conference Office, 1872 |
| WJWB    | The Works of John Wesley. Edited by Frank Baker. Bicentennial Edition. Nashville, TN: Abingdon, 1975– (formerly published by Oxford University Press) |
| WL      | The Word of Life. Thomas C. Oden. San Francisco: Harper Collins, 1989 |
| WML     | Works of Martin Luther: An Anthology. Philadelphia edition. 6 vols. Philadelphia: Muhlenberg Press, 1943 |

# Index

)f
|s
e
g
/;
;-
)f
n
l.
s
)f
.-

...

| DATE DUE | | | |
|---|---|---|---|
| IL 11-4-95 | | | |
| AUG 1 4 1998 | | | |
| DEC 0 3 1998 | | | |
| AUG 05 | | | |
| | | | |
| | | | |
| | | | |
| | | | |
| | | | |
| | | | |
| | | | |

## CONCORDIA COLLEGE LIBRARY
2811 NE Holman St.
Portland, OR 97211